BIKE

FITNESS, FUN & EASY MAINTENANCE

David North. Foreword by Mark Bickerton

**FLAME TREE
PUBLISHING**

Publisher and Creative Director: Nick Wells
Senior Project Editor: Catherine Taylor
Art Director: Mike Spender
Digital Design and Production: Chris Herbert
Picture Research: Laura Bulbeck, Polly Prior, Catherine Taylor
Special Photography: David North

Special thanks to: The Bike Factory, Chester (www.thebikefactory.co.uk); Joseph Kelly and Laura Bulbeck.

FLAME TREE PUBLISHING
6 Melbray Mews, Fulham, London SW6 3NS
United Kingdom

www.flametreepublishing.com

First published 2016

16 18 20 19 17
1 3 5 7 9 10 8 6 4 2

© 2016 Flame Tree Publishing Ltd

A CIP record for this book is available from the British Library upon request.

ISBN 978-1-78664-084-0

Printed in China

The images on pages 65, 142, 145–48, 150–162t, 163 are copyright © Flame Tree Publishing Ltd.

Many thanks to the following for permission to use their images: **Pashley Cycles** 22, 36, 53; **Electra Bicycle Company** 23;
The Moulton Bicycle Company 24; **Tern Bicycles** 25; **www.boardmanbikes.com** 28; **Specialized** 30; **www.thorncycles.co.uk** 33;
Halfords 35t, 41br, 42, 56t, 56br, 149t; **AgainsttheGrind.com** 67; © **Birmingham Monarchs** 136t; **Park Tools** 143.

Courtesy of **Shutterstock.com** and © the following photographers: iofoto 4 & 47, 45; Joe Gough 6, 54l; Monkey Business Images
7, 13, 34; Maxim Petrichuk 8, 171; Barnaby Chambers 9; Deklofenak 12; emberiza 14; Adam Gryko 15 & 37; Vasaleks 16, 29,
132; Dmitry Naumov 17, 27, 32; greenland 18, 108, 109; Jorg Hackemann 19; michaeljung 20; Sue McDonald 21; Eder 26;
steamroller_blues 168b; NizamD 31; Richard Thornton 35b, 168t; Krasi 40; Cathleen A Clapper 41t; Colour 41cr; Imcsike 41bl;
Sean MacD 41cl; Blazej Lyjak 43b, 129; SasPartout 43t; wk1003mike 44b; estike 44t; JinYoung Lee 46; Andre Bonn 48b; Pelham
James Mitchinson 48t; Mariano N. Ruiz 49; adam36 50t; Martin Kemp 50c; STILLFX 50b; m.bonotto 51; Barghest 52t; Bridget
McPherson 52b; Jiri Pavlik 54r; photka 55t; Skoda 55b; Maxim Godkin 56bl; Pavel Kolotenko 57; Ronette vrey 60, 61; Diego Cervo
62; CandyBoxPhoto 63; Eimantas Buzas 64; Roca 66; Radu Razvan 68t; RTimages 68b; Bartlomiej Nowak 71t; THP I Tim Hester
Photography 71b; Fishking 72; Barry Blackburn 73; Olga Danylenko 74; italianestro 75; Rocksweeper 76; John Orsbun 77; SVLuma
78, 83; Vaclav Volrab 79; Anna Grigorjeva 80; Sergiy Zavgorodny 81; Kevin George 82; Volodymyr Baleha 84; VanHart 85; Krkr 86;
RedTC 87; Amy Johansson 88; Steffen Foerster Photography 89; Vicente Barcelo Varona 90; Perig 91; joyfull 94; Calek 95; Hellen
Sergeyeva 96; Stephen Coburn 97; Sunny_baby 98; Igorsky 99; Minerva Studio 100; hairy mallow 101; PARKHYEJUN 102; Rikard
Stadler103; kleyman 104; sianc 105; Nataliya Hora 106; Remus Moise 107; RonGreer.Com 110; Gemenacom 111; Firma V 112;
Dudarev Mikhail 113; Pedro Jorge Henriques Monteiro 116; Cupertino 117; maga 118, 120; Scott Leman 119; Ken Inness 121;
nickpit 122; EPG_EuroPhotoGraphics 123; Timofeyev Alexander 124; Elena Elisseeva 125, 128; Mrakoplas 126; Marcin Balcerzak
127, 173; Yuri Arcurs 130, 169; Chrislofoto 131; Peter Zaharov 133; archetype 134t; Yoree Grozenok 134b; Timothy Large 135;
Rena Schild 136b; Eric Fahrner 137, 138t; testing 138b; HenrikBolin 144; Grzegorz Petrykowski 149c; Zhax 149b; JIPEN 162b;
Alistair Michael Thomas 166; Alexander Chaikin 167; swinner 170; Warren Chan 172.

CONTENTS

FLAME TREE
PUBLISHING

FOREWORD

When I was about eight years old, my father started designing the Bickerton Portable Bicycle, so much of my childhood was spent with drawings and, later, parts of bicycles cluttering up the kitchen table, whilst he perfected the design of the first really 'portable' bike. I should say that in the process he had considered other fantastical mobility solutions such as portable airships; however – fortunately – the bicycle concept won out!

Throughout my teenage years I was involved in the early manufacture, marketing and promotion of his bikes, until the age of 21 when I was deviated from a career in possibly farming or the army, to help run the bike business. Fun and buccaneering times they were, with many a story to be told, but perhaps for another time.

So for the last 30 years I have been involved in the bike business, whilst always enjoying the benefits of cycling myself. At the last count my family of five has at least nine serviceable bikes and quite a few collectors' items, put aside for some greater purpose. Living in Kent, we are lucky enough to have both the flat lands of the Romney Marshes and the beautiful wooded Weald to ride both on road and off road as a family.

Bikes are perhaps one of the great wonders of the modern world, having regularly won awards as the best invention and other such accolades; bikes have even been accorded a reputation for having played a part in the emancipation of women! Importantly, they allow people to travel cheaply, efficiently and using virtually none of our precious resources. Bikes also have the added benefit of contributing to the health of the rider – and not just physically, as riding a bike gets the endorphins going, and the resultant smile is there for all to see.

I am delighted to report that I am not alone in espousing the virtues of the two-wheeled wonder machine. All over the world, governments and cities are supporting the use of cycling. London has recently seen the introduction of the 'Boris Bikes' rental scheme that within six months clocked up about 2.5 million journeys, over a calculated 6.5 million miles, at an average of 10 mph. Motor users, put that in your pipe and smoke it! Also, Transport for London (TfL) is putting in a whole network of 12 radial 'Cycle Super Highways', with at least eight completed and already acting as arterial bike routes for the capital. Perfect also for all the recent commuters who have been able to obtain bikes through one of the many tax-saving Cycle to Work schemes that are now available through their employers.

This book will help you choose the right bike, kit yourself up properly and ride efficiently and safely, and then after getting the most out of your bike, the book will help you to tenderly care for it. *Bike* will give you lasting service and pleasure for years.

Mark Bickerton
Deputy President of the Bicycle Association of Great Britain

INTRODUCTION

Cycling has been an affordable and efficient mode of transport and a popular leisure activity for well over a century. It has seen periods of immense popularity and others of decline. Today we are seeing an upsurge in interest, no doubt due in part to the problems of pollution, congestion and the increasing costs of other forms of transport. However, cycling offers so much more than just a second travel option.

Further to Go

Despite a 40-per-cent increase in the number of adults cycling to work, little more than one per cent of commuters in the UK and US are cyclists. Given that the average commute is little more than 4 km (2.5 miles), there are a huge number of people who could easily join the cycling revolution. Perhaps you are one of them. If so, this book will guide you through everything you need to know. If you are already cycling on a regular basis, you will probably still find much in here to enhance your cycling knowledge and experience.

Popularity

Many people who have taken up cycling in order to save money, reduce their commute or save the environment are discovering that it also offers a far more enjoyable experience in terms of increased health and fitness as well as a sense that what they are doing is, quite simply, a really good thing, for themselves and for the world around them.

The Benefits Package

The many benefits of cycling will be covered in more detail in the next chapter, but a short summary here will give you a taste of what cycling has to offer.

- **Health:** Cycling is so good for you that it actually improves not just your health and fitness but your life expectancy too. People who cycle at a moderate pace for 30 minutes, five days a week have a life expectancy two years longer than people who don't exercise.

- **Pleasure:** It helps you to de-stress and gives your spirits a boost.

- **Natural:** Although a modern technology, cycling feels far more natural than other forms of transport, most likely due to the slower pace and moderate physical effort required.

- **Family and friends:** Cycling is a great way to spend time with your family and friends and enjoy some wonderful days out in beautiful countryside.

- **Speed:** Although moderate cycling uses the same energy as walking, you travel three times faster. For commutes of a few kilometres in urban areas, cycling is often the fastest means of transport.

☼ **Mobility:** Cycling is the most accessible and convenient form of transport other than walking. You don't need a licence and you can go just about anywhere, door to door.

☼ **Sport:** There are many cycle sports that appeal to a very broad cross-section of people.

☼ **Travel:** Cycling is a great way to travel and see places. You travel fast enough to feel that you are getting somewhere, yet slow enough to enjoy the scenery as you go.

☼ **Making friends:** Cycling's many clubs, associations, sporting events and enthusiasts offer a great way to meet like-minded people in a genuinely fun and friendly atmosphere.

☼ **Affordable:** Compared to driving a car, cycling is incredibly cheap and can easily be cheaper than public transport if you buy a moderately priced bike and ride it regularly.

☼ **Transporters:** The right bike with the right extras can easily carry the week's shopping for an average family.

☼ **Public safety:** Cycling rarely causes death or serious injury to pedestrians.

☼ **Environmentally friendly:** Last but certainly not least, bicycles are the greenest form of transport apart from walking. They do not pollute, pump out carbon dioxide, use up vast amounts of resources or kill animals.

About This Book

Whether you are new to cycling or an old hand, I am sure this book will prove a useful guide and resource. It covers quite a broad range of aspects of cycling, but does not go into too much detail on advanced or technical matters – further information on some subjects can be found on our website, for which you will see links throughout the book. In addition to sections on **how to choose** your bike, **what kit** you need, using your bike for **commuting** and **shopping**, keeping it **secure**, **children** and cycling, and cycling for **health**, **fun** and **sport**, there is one chapter that I believe is relevant to every reader and one that would be very useful:

Safe Cycling

Despite cycling being much safer than people realize, I would prefer there to be no accidents at all. To that end I urge you to read this chapter. It also features practical advice on how to ride a bicycle. The skills and techniques presented here are integral to safety, not just comfort and efficiency. Setting off without wobbling, braking correctly, riding in a straight line and signalling clearly are core skills essential to safe cycling.

Bicycle Maintenance

It isn't essential that you maintain your own bicycle – a mechanic can do that for you – but it is important that you can perform certain checks and adjustments as well as clean and lubricate it. Here we look at useful tools and new bike tasks, along with how to repair a puncture – further maintenance tasks and step-by-step instructions can be found at www.flametreepublishing.com/extras.

Enjoy

Whatever adventures you may have on your bicycle, I hope you find this book helpful in making them all the richer and more enjoyable.

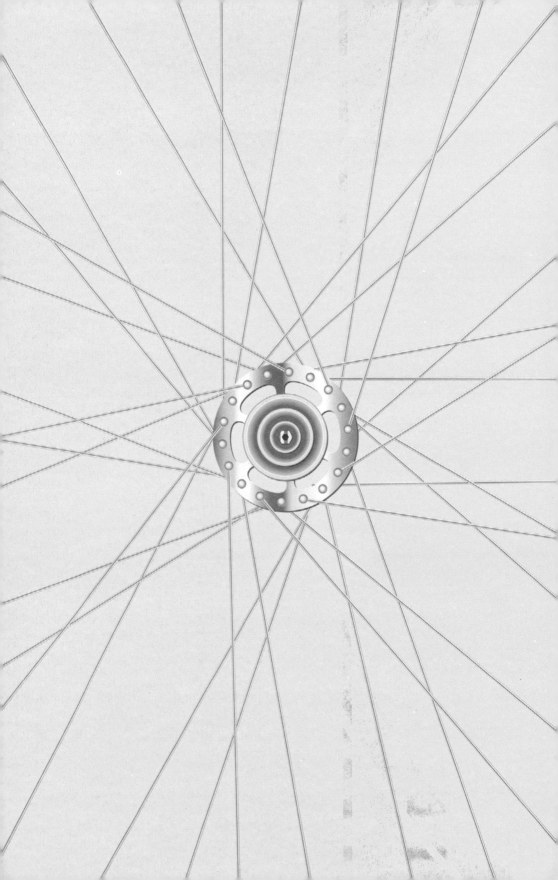

CHOOSING A BICYCLE

WHICH BIKE?

There are so many types of bicycle that finding the right one can be daunting. This chapter will not be able to tell you which bicycle is right for you, but it will help you to narrow the options down from the many to a few.

Different Bikes for Different Jobs

Over 150 years of innovation in bicycle design has produced a profusion of bicycles for every kind of purpose: commuting, road racing, off-road racing, shopping, transporting goods, performing acrobatics, touring the world and more. Before looking at some of these types of bicycle, including those suitable for children, let's consider how to narrow down our options.

Fit for Purpose

Bicycles have become very specialized in recent decades and generally do what they are designed to do very well. But they no longer do other things quite as well or, in some cases, not very well at all. So, the first step is to think about what you will be using your bicycle for.

Multi-purpose Bicycle

Unless you are getting involved in a competitive sport, for which you will want a specialized bicycle, you may well want one that does several different things. Of these different purposes, you will probably want your bicycle to do one of them very well and the others well enough. Such bicycles exist. All you need to do is make a list of the things you will use your bicycle for, with emphasis on the most important aspects, such as getting to work quickly or being able to carry all of your shopping.

Fine Details

The next step is to work out how quickly you want to get to work, how rough the trails are going to be and how much shopping or camping equipment you are likely to take. This is where the bicycle store staff will be able to help, or other cyclists on internet forums. In fact, 99 per cent of the questions you might have will probably have already been asked, and answered, on many a forum. Now you will have narrowed the range to half a dozen or fewer.

Top Tip

You probably won't buy another bicycle for a long time, so spend the most you can afford. You will feel much happier with the bike you actually want rather than one that saved you some money.

Budget

How much have you got to spend? Bear in mind that you will need about 10 per cent of the cost of the bike to spend on locks, and you will also need lights and probably mudguards, a rack, tools, puncture-repair kit and so on (see the next chapter on *Equipment & Clothing*, pages 38–57). With a clear budget in mind, unless you are very well off, you will now have narrowed your options down to just a few.

Bike Size

This is extremely important. It will determine whether you will have a comfortable experience of cycling or one of discomfort, pain and possible injury. It is unlikely to affect your choice, as most models of bicycle are available in a range of sizes, but it will be a critical factor if you decide to buy online or buy a used bicycle, so make sure that you know what the right size is for you. Ideally, go to a bicycle store and try some for size and seek advice from a shop assistant.

The Right Size

For everyday, non-specialist cycling, many bicycles come in clothing-style sizes: small, medium and large, with some offering extra-small and extra-large. If that is the case, they should also give a guide to what those mean in actual centimetres or inches. Having a measurement will give you a more precise fit.

⚙ **Height:** You should have 2.5 to 5 cm (1 to 2 inches) of clearance between you and the crossbar when you straddle the frame with both feet flat on the ground.

⚙ **Length:** This is generally not considered in frame label measurements, but frames do increase in length as they increase in height. If necessary, you can adjust or replace the handlebars to make this more comfortable.

Hybrid and Mountain Bicycle Sizes

This chart is not for road bicycles, which have a different setup. The term 'road bike' refers to specialist bicycles designed for road racing, as opposed to off-road or track racing.

Your Height	Your Inseam Length	Bike Frame Size
4'11"–5'3"	25"–27"	13–15 inches
5'3"–5'7"	27"–29"	15–17 inches
5'7"–5'11"	29"–31"	17–19 inches
5'11"–6'2"	31"–33"	19–21 inches
6'2"–6'4"	33"–35"	21–23 inches
6'4" and up	35" and up	23 inches and up

Seat Height

This is the second stage of sizing once you have the right frame, but it is not a critical factor in the choosing of a bicycle as it is adjustable. However, there can be a significant difference in how it feels to sit on different bicycles of the same frame size and seat height. This will mainly be due to the type of handlebars fitted. Ask the shop assistant to help you with the right height, or read the section on 'Correct Posture' in the *Safe Cycling* chapter on pages 68–69, or page 145 in the *Bicycle Maintenance* chapter.

Buying from a Shop

This is your best option, as you get professional advice, the correct size and the guarantees and warranties that you won't get with a used bicycle. At the very least it is worth visiting a few shops even if you intend to buy a used bicycle or online. After all, advice is free and so is the opportunity to sit on a bicycle and see how it feels.

Buying Online

You can often get better deals through online retailers, or get a bicycle that isn't available in your local shops. Before buying, check the returns policy so that you can return it and get your money back if anything is faulty or even if it just doesn't feel comfortable.

Buying a Used Bicycle

When buying a used bicycle through the internet, there are two important things to remember: the possibility that the bicycle might be stolen; and once you have bought it you probably won't be able to return it unless it is 'not as described'.

Stolen Bicycle for Sale

Before buying a used bicycle, ask the seller if it has been registered and, if so, with whom. Also, ask them to provide a frame number. This is stamped on most bicycles on the underside of the bottom bracket, where the pedals join the frame.

Used Bicycle Checks

If you can get to see a bicycle before you buy it then so much the better. As well as checking it is the right size (see opposite), you should also take it for a test ride to see how it feels and whether the brakes work, anything feels loose, you can hear any creaks or squeaks, and that the gears change smoothly. Ideally you should also check the state of the frame, wheels, tyres, brakes, cranks, chain, sprockets, cables, seatpost, headset – more detailed information on what you need to look for can be found here: www.flametreepublishing.com/extras.

CHILDREN'S BICYCLES

Buying a bicycle for a child is not something to be done casually. Although cycling is a fun activity for children, it is also a potentially dangerous one. If you value your child's safety (and of course you do), make sure you buy a safe bicycle.

Safety First

There are thousands of children's bicycles for sale via all manner of suppliers, including discount stores, catalogues, toy stores and supermarkets. Some of these bicycles might be good, others might not. You can't easily know the true quality of such bicycles and can't be certain that the store knows either. However, bike stores will know a good bicycle from a bad one so, even if you pay extra, buy from a bicycle store.

Bicycle Sizes for Children

Getting the right-sized bicycle for a child is very important, especially as they have a tendency to grow. For this reason some parents are tempted to buy a larger bicycle for the child to grow into. This is not a good idea. When the bicycle is too large, the child will find it more difficult to

control. Moving the seat and handlebars higher will save you having to buy every size of bicycle as the child grows. A bicycle that is slightly too small is preferable to one that is too big.

Basics of Size

A child needs to be able to stand with one leg on either side of the bicycle frame, so make sure that they have a few centimetres of clearance if the bicycle has a crossbar. Unlike the seat height for adults, the height of the seat on a child's bike should allow the rider to touch the ground with the balls of his or her feet when sitting. Also, unlike adult bikes, children's bike sizes are designated by the wheel size in inches.

Size Guide

Children's bicycles start at 12" and rise to 24". As children grow at different rates, choosing a bicycle according to age is not the best method. Ideally, go to a shop with your child or, if buying used, have the child with you to make sure that you get the right size. If buying online, the manufacturer should provide a size chart that will correspond to your child's height and inside-leg measurement.

12" wheel (2 to 5 years)

There are two main types for this age group: ones with pedals and ones without. Those without pedals are learner bicycles for children who are just starting. Having no

Top Tip

As children on bicycles are harder for motorists to see, attach a high-visibility safety flag to your child's bicycle.

pedals allows them to concentrate on balancing, steering and braking. Once they have developed the basic skills, they can progress to a 12" or 14" wheel with pedals. A *good* 12" bike won't cost less than the high double figures.

14" wheel (3 to 6 years)
These are not as commonly available as most of the other sizes, but are useful for fast growers, bridging the gap from 12" to 18". Expect to pay proportionately more than the 12".

16" wheel (5 to 8 years)
This is the age that children will be looking to ride without stabilizers and may even be thinking about 'style'. Many children's bicycles at this size are miniature BMX bikes, mountain bikes (MTB) and road bikes. The MTBs will offer different frame designs and some will even have suspension, which are fashionable but expensive, and probably unnecessary. Some may come with gears. Again, prices are proportionately more than the 14".

18" wheels (6 to 9 years)
As with the 14" wheel, this size is not as widely available as the other children's sizes. Some of these come with five or six gears. The two main advantages of having gears at this stage are that the child begins to learn how to use gears, and he or she is better able to keep up with adults. Again, you pay more for the bigger size.

20" wheels (7 to 10 years)

This is the same size wheel as an adult BMX and could well be the last bicycle the child uses before moving on to an adult size. 20" wheel bikes also introduce more adult styles and features, including disc brakes and up to 18 gears. These are not essential. As long as the bicycle is the right size and has good brakes it will be enough, although you may want it to have some gears, if not as many as 18. Prices again will be relatively higher.

24" wheel (8 to 11 years)

It is quite common to step up from a 20" wheel to an adult-size 26" wheel with a small frame of 14" to 15", but for those children who have outgrown a 16" or 18" wheel, this size could allow them to miss out the 20" wheel. You can also get road (racing) bikes with drop handlebars at this size. Their proximity to adult-size bicycles is reflected in the price, with the price range being wider, depending on the brand and quality.

26" wheel

This is an adult-size wheel for adult-size bikes, but I include it in this list because it is possible to get some mountain bikes with smaller frames, therefore making it possible for some youngsters to skip the 24" wheel.

Other Things to Consider

Having ascertained the right size of bicycle for your child, you will want to consider some other factors before making your purchase.

Weight

Children's bicycles can take a lot of rough treatment so they need to be durable. To do this cheaply, heavier materials are used which, from the child's perspective, could be very heavy and make control of the machine more difficult. It may well be worth paying that little bit extra so your child has a lighter bicycle that is still capable of taking the knocks. For 20" and 24" bikes, don't go higher than 13 kg (28 lb) and aim for less if the child is likely to be cycling on fields or rough tracks, or climbing hills.

Components

⚙ **Brakes:** Make sure that your child can reach the brake levers easily. If they can't be repositioned, they will need to be replaced.

⚙ **Stabilizers:** These should come with all 12" bikes and you can also get them on larger-size bikes up to 16". Ideally, get the bicycle with the stabilizers already fitted.

⚙ **Wheels:** These should be miniature versions of adult wheels, with rims, spokes and tyres. Don't buy anything with plastic wheels.

⚙ **Crank arms:** These are the arms that join the pedals to the bicycle frame. Ideally these should be around 10 per cent of the child's height.

⚙ **Gears:** These are not really necessary, but five or six would be useful for children who have developed competent cycling skills and are regularly tackling hills, or riding with adults. For older children on 18" wheels or higher, more gears would be necessary if they are getting involved in off-road riding or road racing.

⚙ **Suspension:** This is not necessary unless the child is active in an MTB sport. Suspension also adds weight and requires maintenance. If you do choose suspension, go for air-sprung forks. They are lighter and can easily be adjusted to compensate for the growing child's increasing weight.

No Surprises

If you are buying a bicycle, especially for an older son or daughter, then involving them in the process will be better than trying to surprise them. This is not just because of the importance of getting the right size and type of bike, which is especially important for more expensive, performance bikes like road, MTB and BMX, but because many teenagers will have a very good idea of what they want. You might not be able to afford that, but at least you can find compromises rather than buying something that disappoints.

Top Tip

When buying your child a new bicycle, make sure to also buy high-visibility wear with reflective material built in and a very good helmet.

BMX Bikes

BMX (bicycle motocross) was originally designed for racing on dirt tracks. Since then, a 'freestyle' form of BMX has evolved with five disciplines: park, ramp (also known as vert), dirt jump (jump or trail), street and flatland. There are BMX-style bikes with smaller wheels for younger riders, starting at 16" wheels, but a BMX proper has 20" wheels with a frame suitable for a rider measuring 147 cm to 193 cm (4ft 10 in to 6 ft 4in). However, it is possible to get a 20" wheel BMX with a smaller frame that would, therefore, be suitable for a rider shorter than 147 cm (4ft 10 in). Unlike other children's bikes, BMXs are specialized machines with different features for the different disciplines. For a general guide on choosing and buying visit: www.flametreepublishing.com/extras.

ADULT BICYCLES

This section looks at the most common types of bicycle and a few of the less common. Although not a comprehensive review, it will certainly give you a good idea of what is available. The first five types of bicycle are collectively called 'utility bikes' and are designed for uses such as commuting, shopping or transporting goods.

Town and City

The first two bicycles here – the English roadster and the European city bicycle – are both design classics with a long history. They are primarily designed for sedate riding and are particularly good as town and city bikes. That said, I know of people who have used a roadster for touring.

English Roadster Bicycle

These used to be very common in Britain, then faded with the increasing popularity of modern-style bikes. However, they have become very popular around the world and there are signs that they may be making a comeback in the UK. They are elegant bicycles, ideal for leisurely rides around town.

The Roadster Classic by Pashley.

⚙ **Design features:** A modern roadster has a steel frame and generally features a chaincase and coat guards, mudguards, a rear carrier, a leather sprung saddle, a wheel stand and hub brakes (a.k.a. drum brakes; these act on the hub of the wheel rather than on the rim or a disc). Depending on the model they may include dynamo lights. The wheels can be 26" or larger. They will be either single speed or have a three-speed hub gear (hub gears are inside the actual hub of the wheel so are much more discreet than derailleur gears, which are instantly recognizable as the ones that hang down from the rear wheel and have numerous cogs – sprockets – extending in a cone from the hub of the wheel). Built for durability, they are heavy but make good shopping bikes.

European City Bicycle

These are the elegant, curved-frame bicycles usually associated with Amsterdam, although their use is widespread throughout Europe. They are very similar to the roadster in that they are designed for unhurried, urban riding.

The Amsterdam Jetsetter 3i by Electra.

⚙ **Design features:** Many now have alumnium frames, so they can be lighter than a roadster. They also have a chaincase, coat guards, mudguards, a rear rack, sometimes a cushioned saddle, a stand and are single-speed or have three-speed hub gears. They usually have built-in dynamo lights, use either drum or coaster brakes (which require a reverse motion of the pedal to engage them and also act on the hub of the wheel) and the handlebars tend to be higher, leading to a more upright posture. Some also include an inbuilt lock.

Top Tip

Sizes of English roadsters and European city bikes differ from those of hybrids and mountain bikes, so make sure to check the manufacturer's size guides.

Buying a Roadster or European City Bicycle

New roadsters are made by British bicycle manufacturer **Pashley** and aren't the cheapest bikes around. Cheaper 'hybrid' versions by other manufacturers might be called 'classic bikes', 'town bikes' or 'comfort bikes'. European city bicycles (also known as Dutch bikes) are manufactured by **Electra**, the **Dutch Bicycle Company**, **Dutchie** and **Flying Pigeon**. They tend to be somewhat more affordable than Pashley roadsters. There is a hybrid of similar design called a 'city bike'.

Small-wheel and Folding Bicycles

There are a few misconceptions about small-wheel bicycles (less than 26"), so let's clear those up now. Not all folding bicycles have small wheels; not all small-wheel bicycles fold; and not all small-wheel bicycles are for children. Furthermore, they are not inferior to those with larger wheels. On the contrary, cycling pioneer Paul de Vivie said, 'I can guarantee that in an experiment extending as far as 15,000 kilometres covered, they will not have the smallest disadvantage.'

Benefits of Small Wheels

You will probably be surprised just how impressive small-wheel bikes can be. Here are their main advantages:

 Speed: Up to 24 kph (16 mph) the small wheel is more efficient than a 26" wheel and remains on a par with them until 52 kph (33 mph), when the bigger wheel becomes more effective.

The non-folding small-wheel Moulton TSR 2.

⚙ **Control:** Being closer to the ground, with wheels that grip the road better due to their size, it is easier to control and steer the bicycle.

⚙ **Fitting:** You can get a better fit with small-wheel bikes than with larger ones, which is a great advantage if you have a shorter inside leg, or are below average height.

⚙ **Compact:** Being small and light they are much easier to store, so ideal if you live in a flat, take them on a train or in your car, or if it is a folding bike.

⚙ **Strength:** There is no reason for a small-wheel bicycle, whether folding or not, to be weaker than larger-wheel bikes. On the contrary, their compact design can give them excellent strength in relation to weight.

Non-Folding

The classic non-folding small-wheel bicycle is the **Moulton**. Launched in the UK in the 1960s, it fast acquired iconic status. For touring and trekking, **Airnimal** make ones that can be collapsed and easily sent by plane. **Gocycle** make an electric small-wheel bike.

Folding

Although these are generally associated with small wheels, there are manufacturers, like **Dahon** for example, who also make 26" wheel bikes that fold. Another manufacturer, **Montague**, even makes a 26"-wheel, folding bicycle designed to be parachuted into war zones for use by soldiers.

The folding Tern Eclipse X22 from Tern Bicycles is a full-size road bike with 26" wheels.

Buying

Apart from those already mentioned, there are many recognized brands including **Brompton**, **Bike Friday**, **GoBike**, **iXi**, **Dawes**, **Kansi** and more. Prices start relatively low but can become quite eye-watering for the well-known brands.

Mountain Bicycle (MTB)

Sometimes called All Terrain Bicycles (ATB), these are commonly seen on our roads, although this type of bicycle was, and still is, actually designed for off-road use, specifically on very rough terrain. There are cheaper versions that aren't really designed for serious off-road use, but then they aren't really MTBs.

Distinguishing Features

To cope with rugged terrain, MTBs are sturdy, have wide, knobbly tyres for good traction, straight handlebars, multiple gears generally ranging from 16- to 28-speed, good braking systems and, in recent years, offer some form of suspension. Suspension can be at the front only or both front and rear. The former are often referred to as 'hardtails'.

Everyday Use

The popularity of the MTB as an everyday bicycle is probably due to a combination of fashion and the fact that during the 1980s and 1990s their range of gears, strength and ability to cope well on winter roads made it a good choice as an all-round bike. However, there have been developments in recent years to both MTBs and other bicycles, meaning that they are no longer the unrivalled all-rounders they once were.

Top Tip

If you want to use an MTB for commuting, you can fit new tyres designed for road use that will make a noticeable improvement to your speed.

Technological Advances

Modern MTBs have come a long way since their original inception in the 1970s and, as such, have become far more specialized as regards the purpose they were designed for: off-road cycling. This makes them less suited to everyday use when compared with other types of bicycle. MTBs have also instigated many new technologies that have been adopted by other types of bicycle, ones designed to be all-rounders.

Shop Around

Given the specialized nature of MTBs and the developments seen in other types of bicycle, unless you are planning to ride off-road, it is worth giving serious consideration to those other types. If you are getting an MTB for off-road use, you will need to research. There are various MTB disciplines, so there is no single type of MTB. Your first step then is to identify the style of riding you intend to do.

Buying

Given the popularity of MTBs you will not have much trouble finding one. I strongly recommend that you visit your local bike store and talk to MTB enthusiasts to find out more about the different bikes available and their relative merits. As these are not the cheapest end of the spectrum, you will want to make sure that you get the best one for you.

Hybrid Bicycle

Hybrid bikes are a recent design development, drawing on elements of mountain bike and road bike design to produce a more versatile and affordable bicycle for the average cyclist. The hybrid is good for commuting, light trail riding and cycle touring. There are subtypes too, mixing elements of other bicycles like the English roadster and European city bike. Although often classed as utility bikes, I have given them a separate section due to their popularity and availability.

The Boardman Women's Hybrid Comp.

Combined features

A standard hybrid frame utilizes the upright, stronger frames of MTBs and similar handlebars. They use derailleur gears in a similar range to a road bike and, like the road bike, the wheel size is usually larger than an MTB's. However, unlike the road bike, the hybrid's wheel rims are slightly wider for strength. Tyres are less chunky than those of the MTB so better suited to road riding, but will often have a deeper tread than road bikes for trail riding. Higher tyre pressure compared to an MTB makes them faster on the road.

Variants

The following could be called 'subtypes' of the hybrid, as they combine elements of other types of bicycle.

 Trekking bike: This is a hybrid that is fitted with extras for touring such as mudguards, a pannier rack and lights. They also make good commuting and shopping bikes.

- ⚙ **Commuter bike:** This typically features 700c wheels (which are slightly larger than 26" wheels) with lighter tyres than a normal hybrid or trekking bike, derailleur gears, mudguards, a rack, lights and sometimes a chainguard to protect trousers.

- ⚙ **City bike:** This is based on the European city bike but features derailleur gears and a lighter weight frame. The wheels are usually 26" and slightly wider than the European city bike or commuter bike.

Top Tip

You may find that buying a hybrid complete with accessories, like a rack and mudguards, will work out cheaper than having to buy the accessories separately.

- ⚙ **Comfort bike:** This is based on the English roadster and will have derailleur gears, though some have hub gears, a modified MTB frame, angled handlebars for a more upright posture and 26" wheels slightly wider than a roadster's. They may also include front suspension, saddle and seatpost suspension.

Buying

These are great all-round bikes for commuting, shopping and leisure. Think about what you want to use your bike for and what accessories you will need, and then visit a few bikes stores and look online to see what hybrid suits. As these bikes are so accessible they are happily also available at relatively affordable prices, though needless to say you can still spend a lot on top of the range makes should you wish!

Road Bicycle

These are the bikes used in races like the Tour de France, hence the other name they are also known by, 'racing bikes'. Like MTBs they are specialized sports bikes, though people who use them for road racing may well also use them for commuting. After all, they are fast.

Defining Features

Road bikes are notable for their lightweight frames and components, drop handlebars to allow the rider to take a more aerodynamic riding position, narrowly spaced multiple gears, narrow 700c wheels, a narrow saddle and high-pressure tyres to reduce rolling resistance. Being built for speed, they don't come with accessories or the mountings for attaching many.

Things to Consider

Are you going to use your road bike to race or for something else like training, fast commuting or taking part in non-competitive club rides? Identifying the purpose will help you to determine the price, as a focus on racing, for example, will mean that you will want a better, more expensive bike.

 Frames: There are four common types of material used for road-bike frames which, in order of price from lower to higher are: aluminium, steel, carbon fibre and titanium. If you intend to race, then carbon fibre would be a better starting choice or, to save a little on the price, you could use an aluminium frame with carbon forks or seatpost.

The Tarmac Comp Disc road bike from Specialized.

⚙ **Frame size:** Road bikes are sized differently to MTBs and hybrids. Getting the right size for you, which includes the length, is particularly important as you will probably be in the saddle for lengthy periods, and these bikes tend to sacrifice comfort for performance.

⚙ **Components:** Pay attention to the quality of the brakes and gears. You will want the smoothest transitions and most efficient braking you can get. You will also need to make a decision about how many gears you want, their range and whether you want two or three chainrings. Campagnolo, Shimano and Sram are good brands for components such as derailleurs, chains, brakes and pedals.

⚙ **Handling and comfort:** Ideally test ride a few bikes to get a feel for the one that handles best and is most comfortable.

Buying

Road bikes are specialized machines made by numerous manufacturers, ranging from basic to high-performance, so their prices reflect this. Research, ask questions and try before you buy. Join a local road-racing club where you will receive plenty of expert advice.

Touring Bicycle

Bicycle touring involves riding long distances over several or more days. It can involve all manner of road surface and terrain, and can be 'supported' in that you carry very little and pay for accommodation as you go, or it can be 'self-supported', where you carry everything you need, such as camping equipment. Although any type of bicycle could be used, there is a classic design that has evolved for the self-supported touring bicycle.

Features of a Touring Bike

The classic touring bicycle aims to carry a rider with a heavy load, over long distances, reasonably quickly. To that end the main features that have evolved over the decades are:

⚙ **Frame:** To support the weight of equipment, whilst providing shock absorption for the rider, a high-quality steel is the preferred material, particularly Reynolds 525, 725 or 853. Another popular type is chromoly. The chainstays (the two frame tubes running parallel to the chain) are longer so you will be less likely to hit your panniers with your heel as you pedal. Tour frames will have all the relevant fittings for attaching mudguards, racks (front and rear), a pump and several water bottles and may well have internal wiring for dynamo lights.

⚙ **Handlebars:** These have traditionally been drop handlebars, almost, but not quite, identical to those of a road bike. They are favoured, not just for the aerodynamic advantage, but because they offer a range of different hand positions, which are welcome on a long day's ride. Recently a new style of touring bar has been developed. Its 'butterfly' shape also offers the rider multiple hand positions.

⚙ **Gears:** Generally they use at least 21-speed derailleur gears to cope with the luggage and steep climbs, but there is now a shift towards using a high-quality hub gear by German manufacturer Rohloff. These, however, are expensive.

⚙ **Wheels and tyres:** Traditionally these have been the larger 700c wheels with smooth road tyres for the benefit of speed. 26" wheels are also used for expedition cycling where rougher roads are expected. Also, 26" wheels are more commonly available around the world, so a cycle tourist going to Africa or Asia may favour a 26" wheel, as it will be easier to find a replacement. Whichever size, they should be strong.

Top Tip

Most bike shops won't be as knowledgeable about touring bikes as they are about the more common types of bicycle. Get some books or research online. Cycle touring forums are a great place to ask for advice.

Buying

Manufacturers include: **Dawes**, **Trek**, **Sakkit**, **Ridgeback**, **Koga-Miyata**, **Thorn**, **Roberts Cycles**, **Condor** and **Giant**. Prices will start fairly high and rise into the thousands.

The Thorn Sherpa touring bike

Other Types of Bicycle

The bicycles covered in this chapter are the main ones in general use, but there are many more variants of this wonderful machine.

Tandem

Tandems are bicycles that can carry two or more people and are a popular choice for cycle touring and families. Riding a tandem takes a little getting used to, so if you get the opportunity to try before you buy then take it. Good bike shops and manufacturers know this, so are happy to let you take a test ride. There are plenty of manufacturers, including **Mission**, **Longstaff**, **Orbit**, **Longbikes**, **Da Vinci**, **Cas**, **Co-Motion**, **Barcroft** and **Greenspeed**. Prices range from pretty cheap to into the thousands.

Electric

Electric bikes, also known as e-bikes, are bicycles with an electric motor for power-assisted pedalling. Most of the common bicycle manufacturers produce e-bikes, as do many specialist

*The Urbanmover
UM44 Usprite
electric bike.*

manufacturers. Prices range from very cheap for
basic models with heavy lead-acid batteries to
exceedingly expensive for modern designs with
lightweight lithium-ion batteries.

Recumbent

Also known as **bents**, these are designed for a
rider to sit in a reclining position with the pedals
in front. This lower, laid-back posture can be
more comfortable than sitting upright, and is also
much more aerodynamic, making them very fast
machines. There are many manufacturers, including
Lightfoot, **Barcroft**, **Easy Racer**, **Linear
Recumbent**, **Ice**, **KMX**, **Giant**, **Longbikes**,
Challenge Bikes and **Windcheetah**. Expect
to pay 10 to 15 per cent more than you would
for an upright bicycle of similar quality.

Special-needs Bicycles

Wheelchair tandems, passenger-carrying bicycles, low step-through frames, electric trikes, hand-pedalled recumbents, hand-pedalled bikes and trikes, wheelchair attachments and one-handed handlebar controls, amongst many other innovations, all exist to enable those who can't easily ride a traditional bike to join in the fun. There is a great buyer's guide that you can download for free at www.velovision.com/mag/issue11/specialneeds150.pdf.

Sports Bicycles

Mountain biking and road racing are not the only cycle sports. There are others such as cyclo-cross, speedway and track, each requiring bicycles designed for those particular sports. The best way to go about buying such a bicycle is to join a club for the relevant sport. They often loan bicycles to new members and, if you find you like the sport enough to buy a new bicycle, they are the best people to advise you.

Cargo Bicycle

With the growing interest in living a greener life and saving on fuel and vehicle costs, the cargo bicycle is making a comeback. For those wanting to exchange the car for something that will still transport a family and its shopping they are an ideal alternative. Many manufacturers are now creating amazing variations that take advantage of modern technologies. Visit the following link to find out more about them: www.flametree publishing.com/extras.

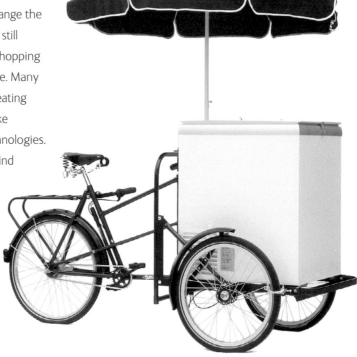

The Pashley Classic No. 33 – an example of a cargo bike that is used to carry goods for sale, such as ice cream.

CHECKLIST

⚙ **Purpose:** Think about all the things you will want to use your bicycle for and make a list of them in order of importance.

⚙ **Bike store:** Visit a bike store and talk to an assistant about the types of bicycle that will best suit your needs. Be prepared to revise your list and look at bicycles you might not have considered.

⚙ **Research:** Visit online forums for cyclists who are doing the things you want to do, and ask for their advice.

⚙ **Budget:** Consider how much you have to spend, bearing in mind that you will probably have to buy equipment too. Some more expensive bikes that come with all the accessories you need may work out cheaper.

⚙ **Aim high:** If you are going to use your bicycle regularly, or for a specific activity like sport or touring, allow the largest possible budget you can afford. You won't buy a bicycle often so get the best you can.

⚙ **Size:** When you have a good idea of the type of bicycle you want, make sure to check what the right size is for you.

⚙ **Details:** Check the details such as frame material, the quality of components, whether there is provision for attaching accessories, number of gears and so on.

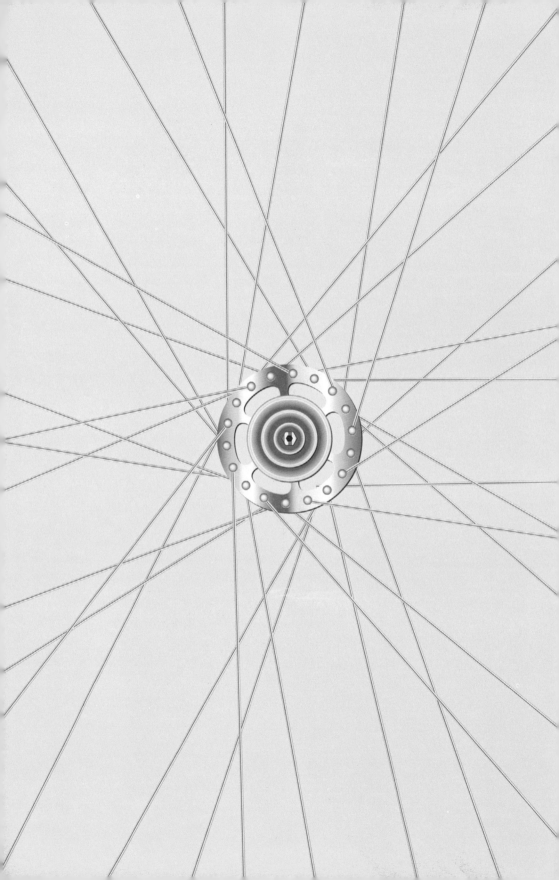

EQUIPMENT & CLOTHING

MORE THAN JUST A BIKE

Once you have bought your new bicycle you could easily ride off without a care in the world – until the sun sets of course, then you'll need some lights and a high-visibility jacket. If you decide to stop for a celebratory drink at a bar or café, and want a bike to ride home, you'll need a lock to secure it. That's right, you are going to need some extras.

Too Much Choice

You could probably open a hypermarket dedicated solely to bicycle clothing and equipment, there's so much of it, and browsing around a bike store can be the cause of such temptation that you really shouldn't enter one with a credit card on your person. So, to spare you any impulsive and unnecessary purchases, the following guide will help you to work out what you need and what you don't.

Top Tip

When budgeting for a new bicycle, don't forget to include a budget for the essential items of high-visibility wear, lights, helmet and lock. The rest you can acquire over time.

Essential and Useful

To make it easier for you to choose what to buy first, I am dividing the chapter into two parts; the first for those items that I believe are essential and the second for those items that will be very useful to have.

Checklists

The following are checklists for all the items I am recommending. I will discuss each one in more detail in the following sections.

Essential Items

- High-visibility wear
- Lights
- Helmet
- Bicycle lock

Useful Items

- Puncture-repair kit
- Bicycle pump (tyre inflator)
- Tools
- Degreaser and lubricant
- Mudguards
- Water carrier
- Bell
- Pannier rack/basket
- Bags
- First-aid kit
- Sunglasses
- Rainwear
- Gloves
- Padded shorts

ESSENTIAL ITEMS

I consider these essential because three of them are the main items of safety equipment for a cyclist and the fourth is the single most important item you could buy to prevent your bicycle, or parts of it, from being stolen.

High-visibility Wear

Personally, I think this is the most important safety feature for a cyclist, even more important than a helmet. If you are seen, you won't be hit, but if you are hit then a helmet won't necessarily save you. Be seen, be safe. It's that simple. It's also very cheap to achieve.

Bright is not Enough

At the very least, bright colours should be worn when cycling during the day, but fluorescent material is better. However, you may be surprised to know that fluorescent material does not work effectively in the dark.

Top Tip

Wrap a piece of 3M Scotchlite tape around the front tube under the handlebars, and another around the seatpost beneath the saddle. This gives 360-degree visibility.

Reflect

What you need for cycling in low light and darkness is reflective material. 3M Scotchlite is excellent and is often fitted to many garments and cycle accessories like panniers. You can also buy it as a self-adhesive roll and attach it to items of clothing and equipment, or make it into simple armbands, wristbands and trouser clips.

Lights

On the subject of being seen, you absolutely must have good lighting and not just for night use. Use them at dawn and dusk, and in the daytime for mist, fog, or overcast conditions. You will need at least one clear light (not red) for the front, which helps you to see as well as be seen, and one red light for the rear. That's the easy part. Now it's just a case of choosing from the huge selection of lights available.

Choosing the Right Lights

There are various factors to consider beyond that of brightness, so you will need to look into the subject in a little more detail. The best thing to do is visit a few bike stores and seek the advice of the assistants. Before doing so, here are some of the things you will need to consider:

- ⚙ **Purpose:** For urban cycling, where there is street lighting, your lights need not be as powerful as those for country lanes or off-road cycling. Flashing front and rear lights are good to use in such areas, especially if switched on in low light or at dawn and dusk, thus allowing you to be seen more easily, with a second, bright front light for illuminating the road ahead when it gets fully dark. For country lanes and tracks you will need a bright front light.

A bottle dynamo.

⚙ **Power:** Most lights are battery powered, some being rechargeable. If you want to do your bit for the environment, I recommend using a dynamo. This converts energy from the rotation of your wheels into electricity. There are two types of dynamo: bottle and hub. Hub dynamos are considered to be much better than bottles, but they are more expensive as you need to buy a wheel with the dynamo installed. Modern hub dynamos are highly efficient and good dynamo lights will emit light for several minutes even when you stop.

⚙ **Types:** There are four main types of bicycle light: LED, Xenon, Krypton and Halogen. Each has its particular advantages and disadvantages. They will use different types of battery (some are rechargeable via USB), use different amounts of power, emit different levels of brightness and different beams of light e.g. narrow or wide. Cheaper lights will generally be fine for riding in the city where there is street lighting, but once you are on to country lanes or cycle tracks you will need a brighter front light.

A front LED light.

Fitting: Different lights have different mountings, so make sure that the lights you want will fit your bicycle. Some lights will attach to various parts of your bicycle, so could well be useful if you later fit a shopping basket and need to move the light from the handlebar to the fork. You will also want lights that are secure in their mounting and won't be shaken out of place by the movement of the bicycle. Some lights have clips or straps that will attach just about anywhere on your bicycle or to your helmet.

Portability: Check that the lights you buy are easy to remove from your bicycle when you leave it and are easy to store in your bag.

Durability: Look for durable lights and mounts made of plastic that won't crack when attaching and detaching the light, or in the cold of winter.

Helmet

The jury is still out on the benefit of helmets, with some claiming that they can, in certain accidents, do more harm than good. Research has also found that people wearing helmets feel safer so ride with less caution, whilst drivers pass cyclists who are wearing helmets more closely. Finally, children have been injured and even killed whilst wearing their cycle helmets for play. However, the fact is that there is enough research to show that helmets generally make a difference in an accident, giving some extra protection to your head and brain.

Top Tip

If you are using battery-powered lights, make sure to carry a spare set with you as their power can fade very quickly, suddenly leaving you in the dark.

My View

If you are visible, have learnt your riding skills properly, know the Highway Code, are aware of the potential hazards, and have a well-maintained bicycle, the chances of you being hit by a car are vastly reduced. However, you still might get hit, or skid on some oil or collide with a pedestrian who stepped off the kerb without looking. This is why I wear a helmet. It is a backup if all else fails.

Choice of Helmets

Some people are put off wearing a helmet by their appearance, usually looking like something from a sci-fi movie. Also, as helmets are generally designed for particular types of riding, some riders who commute and do off-road or sport cycling don't want to have to buy two different helmets. The good news is that there are many styles and types of helmet available. There are helmets that will do the job whether you are riding a mountain bike trail or commuting to work, and several companies produce helmets with the fashion-conscious in mind.

Standards

More important than fashion, however, is function. No matter how good it looks, don't buy it if it does not display a safety standard. For the UK this is written as BS EN 1078:1997, which is the same as the European standard EN 1078:1997. In the US it is the CPSC standard. The independent Snell B90 and B95 standards are considered to be higher than the US and European standards.

Helmet Fitting

Even if you plan to buy your helmet online, first go to a bike store and ask for assistance with the correct fitting and size. Pay attention to the following three aspects:

- **Size:** The helmet should fit comfortably all the way around your head.

- **Straight:** A helmet is designed to be worn low on the forehead, just above your eyebrows.

- **Strap:** Make sure that the chinstrap fits properly, around your ears and under your chin. It should keep the helmet from slipping on your head.

If you can't find a helmet you like in a local bike store, it is still worth trying helmets on to get a good idea of your size. With that information you can then search online for a helmet you do like. Most online sellers will provide a size guide, but make sure before buying that the seller will allow you to return the helmet if it doesn't fit properly.

Never buy a 'used' helmet or even one that might have been used. Slight, imperceptible damage to a helmet can render it useless. Always buy new.

Bicycle Locks

Locking your bicycle is the best way to prevent it from being stolen. An unlocked bicycle left in public probably wouldn't be there for longer than ten minutes. However, even locks can be broken, so when considering locks I recommend that you buy two different types of a high quality.

Types of Lock

The two kinds of lock I recommend are a shackle lock, the most common of which is a 'U lock', and a cable lock. Both require different bulky tools to break, thereby reducing the risk of theft as the thief is most likely to be carrying only one type of tool. Two locks also take longer to break through than one. A good chain lock is an option but they can be very heavy. They are ideal for those who commute regularly by bike as the lock can be left attached to the bike stand overnight.

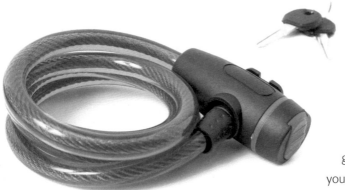

Anchor Lock

Strictly speaking, these are not locks. They are mountings that you attach to your wall or floor if you keep the bicycle outside, in a shed or a garage. You can then secure your bicycle to the anchor using your bicycle lock.

Assessing Lock Quality

Price is often a good indicator, with the more expensive locks being better. Companies will rate their own locks and bicycle shop staff will be able to advise you. Perhaps the best method is to visit the Sold Secure website. Sold Secure conducts independent tests on locks, rating them gold, silver and bronze for their respective ability to withstand attempts to break them.

USEFUL ITEMS

These are not listed in any particular order of importance, though some will be more useful to you than others. They are ordered generally, starting with tools, then accessories and finally clothing.

Puncture-repair Kit

You can decrease your chances of getting a puncture by fitting better-quality tyres and inner tubes with puncture-protection features, or use protective inserts or gels. However, they will not be absolutely puncture proof, so it is worth carrying a repair kit, just in case. There are two options:

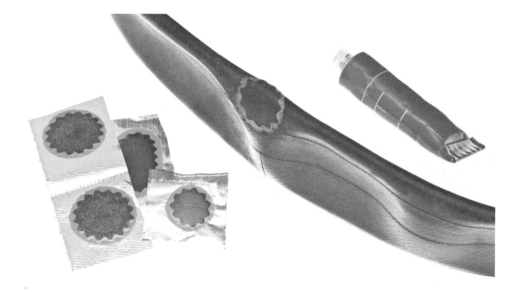

⚙ **Instant fix:** You can buy sprays that inflate your tyre and seal a puncture at the same time. I have never used these, but they do seem like they would be very handy on a dark, wet night. However, I noticed on the container of one brand that it was only good for punctures of 2 mm.

⚙ **Traditional fix:** This involves covering the puncture hole with a patch. Your kit should contain tyre levers, patches, glue (if they are not self-adhesive patches), emery cloth and possibly some chalk. These kits are cheap, small, light and easy to carry.

Bicycle Pumps

Frame pumps are easily attached to your bicycle and hand- or mini-pumps can be attached or carried in a bag. These are great for on-the-spot tyre inflation, but can be hard work and only a few have a pressure gauge. The easiest pump to use is a track pump with a pressure gauge, but they are too big to carry around, so it is best to get a track pump and a portable one.

A Presta valve on an inner tube.

Valves

Bicycles use either a Presta valve or a Schrader valve. You will need to identify which type of valve your bicycle uses and buy the appropriate tyre pump, although you can get adapters.

Tools

Before buying tools you should consider how much maintenance you want to do. It might also be worth looking through your home or car toolbox, as you may already have many of the tools you require for a bicycle. Pages 142–44 in the *Bicycle Maintenance* chapter list the individual tools that you are likely to need for basic maintenance.

A Schrader valve.

Minimal Maintenance Kit

You will need a flat-head screwdriver, a Phillips screwdriver, and a set of Allen keys, also known as Hex keys: sizes 2, 3, 4, 5, 7 and 8 mm. If your bicycle does not have quick-release wheels, or there are nuts that do not take Allen keys, then you will need a spanner or spanners of the appropriate size. Park Tools are a reputable, bicycle tool manufacturer and produce an 'essential tool kit'.

Bicycle Multi-tool

Allen keys and two screwdrivers will allow you to do the majority of basic maintenance tasks on most modern bikes. You can get bicycle multi-tools that contain most, if not all the Allen keys you need and two screwdrivers, whilst other, more advanced multi-tools can feature a crank tool, spanners and chain tool.

Top Tip

If your bicycle has a variety of different-sized nuts, a 150-mm (6-inch) long adjustable spanner with an opening capacity of 20 mm would be an ideal addition to your tool kit.

Degreaser and Lubricant

It is very important to lubricate the moving parts of your bicycle so that they keep moving. It will also prolong their life and save you money in the long run. This is especially true of the chain. Before applying lubricant to the chain, or any other part, you should first clean it. For the chain this is best done with degreaser. Use lubricants and degreasers that are specifically designed for bicycles. Green Oil produce environmentally friendly lubricant and degreaser.

Mudguards

Give some thought to mudguards if you expect to ride in all sorts of weather. Mudguards cover your wheels to protect you and parts of your bicycle, like your saddle, from water and road dirt thrown up by the wheels. They are usually made of metal or durable plastic, and should be purchased according to the size of your wheel.

Wheel Size

This is important to know, not just for your mudguards but also for replacement tyres and inner tubes. You will find the size of yours

written on the side of the tyre. Confusingly, measures vary. However, all you need do is jot down the numbers on your tyre, for example, 26x2, or 700c, or 54-559, and then search for mudguards that are designed for that size. SKS are a popular and reasonably priced make that come in a range of sizes. Mudguards are generally easy to install. See page 147 in the *Bicycle Maintenance* chapter.

Water Carrier

For short trips this is not necessary. For cycle rides of an hour or more, it is important that you have access to water. You can buy frame-mounted water bottles or hydration packs that you wear as a backpack and drink from through a straw. Your bicycle may have some holes in the frame tube, which are for attaching a water carrier for a bottle. However, you don't have to use them or even have them to begin with, as you can get bottle carriers that attach to the frame with their own mounting system.

A Bell

I recommend getting one of these, or some other sound-emitting device, as it is a useful safety device and, although it is unlikely to be loud enough to alert a car driver, it will be enough for warning pedestrians. You can also use a bell as you approach another cyclist before overtaking them.

Pannier Rack/Basket

As you may well end up carrying tools, sunglasses, rainwear, a pump, a water bottle and lights, you'll need somewhere to put them all, not to mention carrying the shopping and your laptop. The way to approach this is to work out what you are likely to be carrying and then allow for extra. Many people use an ordinary backpack. This is fine for shorter distances and light loads,

but over longer distances you run the risk of back injury
and may have your balance affected. As you are
on a machine designed for carrying things,
why not make your life easier and use it?

Choosing a Carrier

You can attach a shopping basket to the
handlebars that will hold a backpack or
shopping bags, or you can attach a rack to the
back that will carry the same, and more. Rear racks
will allow you to put things on top of them, secured
with bungee cords, and also suspend panniers from them.

Top Tip

**If you are planning on
touring, but don't have a touring
bicycle with long chainstays, buy
a longer rack like the Tubus
Logo so you don't hit your
panniers with your heel
as you pedal.**

Installation

This is generally very straightforward once you have identified the right basket or rack for
your bicycle.

☼ **Frame-mounted racks:** These need at least one hole in your frame near where the
rear wheel attaches. You may have two holes in this area, one for a rack and one for a
mudguard. If you only have one hole, you can still use it to attach both a mudguard and
a rack. Some bikes have mountings for racks at the top of the forks below the saddle.
If you don't have them, you will need a rack that comes with a mounting system.
See also page 147 in the *Bicycle Maintenance* chapter.

⚙ **Seatpost-mounted racks:** These do not require any existing mountings on your bicycle. They are attached at one point beneath your seat. You will need to get the right size for your seatpost. They can carry surprising amounts of weight and with a frame can carry panniers. However, I am not aware of them being as good as frame-mounted racks for carrying panniers, so if you have the choice, I would recommend frame-mounted.

⚙ **Baskets:** These should be supplied with handlebar mounts and tend to just slot over the bars without the need for any nuts or screws.

Top Tip

If you put anything on the top of a pannier rack, such as a backpack, make certain that no straps are hanging down or could fall down into your wheels.

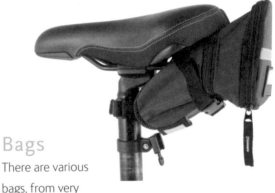

Bags

There are various bags, from very small tool-kit bags to large-capacity touring bags, that attach to different parts of the bicycle.

⚙ **Tool bags:** For your essential tool kit and puncture-repair kit you will only need a small bag. You can buy ones that attach to different parts of the bicycle frame, or to the handlebars, the saddle if your saddle has the attachments for it, or to the seatpost directly beneath the saddle. If you choose to get panniers, you could carry the tools in there, but it is worth keeping them in their own bag so you can locate them easily.

⚙ **Larger bags:** These can attach to the same places as tool bags but, being larger, can carry tools and other items like your gloves, sunglasses, phone, money, camera and the like. Some will have shoulder straps, so you can carry them with you when you leave your bike. Ortlieb and Carradice are good makes.

⚙ **Panniers:** These are the largest bags for a bicycle and usually attach to a rack on the back, although, for long-distance cycle tours, rear panniers can be supplemented with front ones. They can range considerably in price. The more expensive ones are for people who intend to tour. Again, Carradice and Ortlieb are popular choices of pannier for bicycle tourists. A single pannier is often enough for commuting and if you don't want to spend much then don't buy waterproof, just line cheaper panniers with plastic bags.

First-aid Kit

For everyday use this only need contain some antiseptic and gauze dressing for scrapes. For touring you will need a travel-size kit.

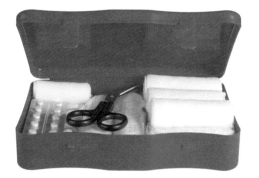

Sunglasses

These are more important than you might think. You need the best visibility possible when cycling and having the sun in your eyes, or light reflecting off a wet road, can be blinding. You can use your regular sunglasses, but if they are not wraparound, you may find that light comes in behind them and reflects back into your eyes, reducing your peripheral vision. If your sunglasses do this, buy a new pair for cycling.

Rainwear

If you wish, you can buy jackets and overtrousers that are specially designed for cycling, and overshoes. However, if you already have breathable rainwear, it should be fine, or you could buy some cheaper rainwear if you only expect to be in the rain infrequently and for short periods of time. Just make sure to wear something reflective over the top and get some bicycle clips if the overtrousers are loose at the bottom.

Cycling-specific Rainwear

The main features that distinguish cycling rainwear
from ordinary rainwear are:

⚙ **Jackets:** They should be breathable, have
a 'fish tail' cut to the back of the jacket so
it hangs over the back of the bicycle seat
and they should have reflective material
like 3M Scotchlite built into the design.

⚙ **Overtrousers:** They should be breathable
and have fastenings on the ankles to prevent
them catching in your chain; ideally they should
also have reflective material built into the design.

⚙ **Overshoes:** If you don't intend to leave your
good shoes at work or carry them on your bicycle,
overshoes will be useful for protecting your shoes
on wet days.

Gloves

Padded cycling gloves are
good if your hands get sore
from leaning on the bars, and
any gloves are essential for cold
weather. You can use your normal gloves, but make sure they are either waterproof or won't
affect your hands if they do get wet. I use a pair of Giro cycling gloves that are great even when
they are wet. For very cold weather, you will need winter gloves, but they should not be so
heavily padded that they affect your ability to operate your gear shifters and brakes.

Padded Shorts

If your saddle is causing you discomfort, you can buy shorts with padding, underwear with
padding or, if you don't like the Lycra look, there are regular-style trousers that are padded.

CHECKLIST

⚙ **Fit for purpose**: Even before buying your bicycle, consider what extra equipment you might need, like a rack or basket, and see if the bicycle you have in mind can accommodate these.

⚙ **Budget for the extra**: Before buying a bicycle, check what equipment you will need to buy straight away, such as locks, lights and safety wear, as you will need to account for them in your budget.

⚙ **Keep it safe**: When buying locks make sure you are able to secure both wheels, as thieves will steal them if they can. Two locks are always better than one.

⚙ **Keep yourself safe**: Make sure to get good lights and some high-visibility clothing, so that you are seen by other road users.

⚙ **Use your head**: Try helmets on before you buy and make sure that the one you get is a good fit.

⚙ **Keep it working**: A puncture-repair kit and some basic tools will make the difference between being stranded and getting home.

⚙ **Carry all**: Think about how much you will need to carry.

⚙ **Any weather**: Be prepared come rain or shine with rainwear and sunglasses.

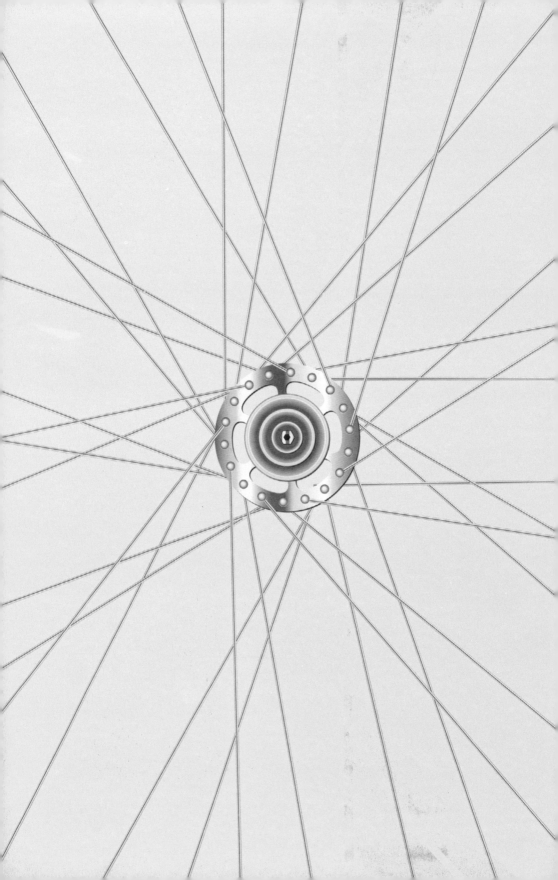

SAFE CYCLING

HOW TO RIDE A BICYCLE

Now that you have a bicycle, and all of your accessories, you will be keen to get on the road and start enjoying all those wonderful benefits that cycling has to offer. Not so fast though. You may need to read this chapter first to find out if you really know how to cycle properly and safely.

Easy as Riding a Bike

The idea that riding a bicycle is easy is a deceptive one. As most of us learnt to ride a bike when we were children, it has become second nature to us. However, much of what we learnt was actually bad habits. We generally don't realize this, because we still manage to get from A to B without incident. However, there are basic cycling skills that are considered the correct way to cycle and, more to the point, will help maintain your health, safety and comfort, not to mention improve your efficiency.

Mounting and Setting Off

You may have noticed that when you set off on a bike you wobble a little. This is because you need a certain momentum to ride in a straight line. Learning the correct starting technique will enable you to reach this momentum much sooner than you probably currently achieve.

Before You Go

Remember that you need to be in the right gear for starting off, so before coming to a stop you need to shift into this gear. It shouldn't be a strain to start off, as this will also cause you to wobble, but nor do you want to be in such a low gear that the pedal doesn't feel like it's there. Practise the following starting and stopping techniques in a safe area, and find the right start-up gear for you. Think quick and smooth.

1. Holding the handlebars with both hands, tip the bike towards you, then lift your knee up and put your leg over the other side. In other words, don't swing your leg over the saddle, especially if there is traffic on the road. You might clip the saddle and lose your balance or, worse, have your leg caught by a passing vehicle.

2. You are now standing, straddling the frame with both feet flat on the ground and, more importantly, you are not sitting on the saddle. This is important for two reasons: firstly, you will be more stable with your feet on the ground; and secondly, you will get more starting power from a standing position.

3. Imagine the circle the pedals make as a clock with 12 o'clock being the top and six o'clock being the bottom. On the side of your weaker leg, position the pedal at two o'clock. This is the side you will start off from.

4. Check for traffic and, when you have the clearest space possible, press forward on the pedal, lift yourself into the saddle and get your other foot on to its pedal. This will give you a good launch speed and get you straight into your riding position. Continue to pedal as described in the Pedalling section over the page.

Stopping and Dismounting

1. Under normal riding conditions, as opposed to emergency stops, downshift to the gear that is the best one for starting off. Make this a habit whenever you are coming to a stop. See the section on 'Changing Gear' on page 64.

2. As you apply your front brake and are almost at a stop, lift yourself off the seat with your weight on the traffic-side pedal, which will be at the six o'clock position.

Top Tip

Before setting off, check that you have the clearest space possible between passing vehicles, just in case you have a wobbly start.

3. Don't put your other foot down until the bike is stopped or as good as. The reason for this is that the bike will stop quicker than you and could throw you off balance, or you may crunch a sensitive area of your body on the crossbar or handlebars.

4. As with mounting, and for the same reasons, dismount by lifting your traffic-side leg up and over rather than swinging it back and over the saddle.

Pedalling

Contrary to what you may think, efficient pedalling is not a matter of making your legs work hard, up and down like pistons. There is a more efficient way to do it.

The Oval Clock

Imagine your legs moving through an oval rather than a circle. Push forward from 11 o'clock to two o'clock, then push down to five o'clock, and then scrape your foot straight back through to seven o'clock. You can practise the technique in a safe area concentrating on just one pedal at a time until each leg gets used to it.

Pedalling Speed

Cadence is a term used for the speed at which you turn the pedals. Most cyclists tend to think that pushing hard in a higher (harder) gear is the way to do it. This results in a slow cadence, not to mention aching legs, hard work, sweat and possibly knee injury. A high cadence in a lower gear is much easier and more efficient. The effort of cycling should be no greater than that of walking.

Top Tip

If you want to measure your cadence properly, you can buy a mini-computer that attaches to your bike and tells you exactly how fast you are pedalling.

The Right Cadence

A good cadence is 80 to 100 revolutions per minute, but counting that isn't easy. Aim to cycle so that the pedals turn quickly but the effort to do so is comfortable, not too loose and without too much resistance. You should never need to strain unless you are climbing a steep hill or riding into a strong wind. Steep hills and strong winds aside, your cadence will remain the same, unless you want to increase the speed by upping a gear.

Changing Gear

Because roads are rarely flat for long, and the wind doesn't always blow in the same direction, and traffic lights, junctions and crossings pop up on a regular basis, in order to maintain your cadence, you will need to change your gears frequently. Here's how gears work (see also page 149 in the *Bicycle Maintenance* chapter for more descriptions of parts of a bike).

The Sprockets

This is the technical name for the cogs that the chain interfaces with. The ones next to your pedals, of which you can have one, two or three, are called chainrings. The ones on your rear wheel are collectively referred to as the cogset. Sometimes they might be referred to as a 'freewheel' or a 'cassette'. The lowest gear, which is the 'easiest' of all, is when your chain is on the smallest chainring and the largest sprocket of the cogset.

The Derailleurs

Most bikes have derailleurs, which are the mechanics that move the chain from one sprocket to another. If you only have one chainring, you will not have a front derailleur. Otherwise, the front derailleur is attached to the bicycle frame immediately above your pedals. Its most obvious component is a long metal cage surrounding the chain above the chainrings. The rear derailleur hangs beneath the cogset. As you move the gear-shift levers on your handlebars, these devices move right or left, pushing the chain on to the next sprocket.

Shift Sequence

To shift up one gear from the lowest, use your rear gear-shift lever to move the chain to the next sprocket on the cogset. To keep moving up one gear at a time, continue to use the rear gear-shift lever. To shift up higher still, use your front gear-shift lever to move the chain on to the next chainring. The highest gear is when the chain is on the largest chainring and the smallest sprocket of the cogset.

Shifting Technique

Find a safe, traffic-free place and practise moving through as much of your gear range as possible, feeling the differences between the gears. As you will probably be on flat ground and only practising, don't expect to use the higher gears. These will be too hard to use. Once you feel familiar with progressive changes, you can make bigger shifts between gears if you have more than one chainring.

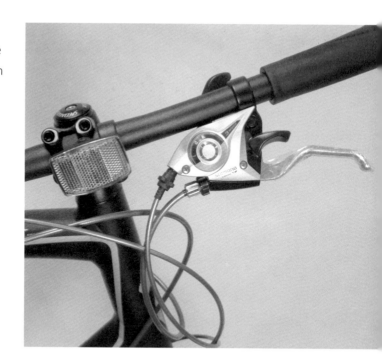

Big Shifts

To make big shifts you only need to shift the front gear. For example, if you have five rear sprockets and you are in your second gear, by shifting up with the front gear only, you will have jumped to your seventh gear. This is most useful when you are coming to a stop. If you are in a high gear and need to stop quite quickly, you can jump five or more gears down so that you will be in an easier start-up gear.

Top Tip

If you are not comfortable with the type of gear-shift mechanism you have, you can have them changed quite easily. Talk to your local bike store about the alternatives.

Braking

As a bicycle slows down weight is transferred to the front wheel, giving it more traction. This makes the front wheel less likely to skid. However, too much power on the front brake alone can cause the bike to tip up and the rider to be thrown on to, or over, the handlebars. Therefore, the best braking technique, for normal road conditions, is where about 75 per cent of the stopping power is applied to the front brake and 25 per cent to the rear brake.

Braking on Slippery Surfaces

In slippery conditions it is better to travel more slowly than you normally would and use the rear brake more than the front. Avoid locking the brakes, as this will cause the wheel to skid. By travelling more slowly, if a skid were to happen, you would be in a much better position to control it.

Bends

Don't brake on bends. Brake before you reach them. Even if you are travelling too fast just before reaching a bend, you will have time to touch and release the brakes and take a slightly wider angle, if it is safe to do so, then lean more into the bend.

Know Your Brakes

Brakes are the one feature of a normal bicycle dedicated solely to safety and for obvious reasons, so, if you get a new bike don't rush on to the road with it but take it to a safe, traffic-free area and get used to your brakes.

Signalling

There are several signals that you can use but, as most are not normally used by cyclists, the majority of motorists are unaware of their meaning, so I shall only cover the main one: turning. Extend your left or right arm for left and right turns respectively. The arm should be straight out from your shoulder. (In the US and Canada another way of signalling to turn right is to extend your left upper-arm out to the left, parallel to the road and then to angle your forearm vertically upward).

Easier Said than Done

It seems simple but there are other factors to bear in mind. Initially you will need to look over your shoulder so that you don't extend your arm into an upcoming vehicle. You will also need to look again as you approach your turn, change gear and brake. This is made more complicated for right turns (left if you are riding in a right-hand drive country), as the front brake lever is usually positioned on the left. The following is something that you can practise in a quiet place.

How to Signal

How you signal will depend on the circumstances and nature of the turn. Ideally, when you are a good way from making your turn, check over your shoulder and also note the oncoming traffic, slow the bike, drop some gears and then, after checking over your shoulder again, make your signal. If you need to slow more, or drop some more gears, you can withdraw your signalling arm and extend it again when you are just a few metres from making the turn.

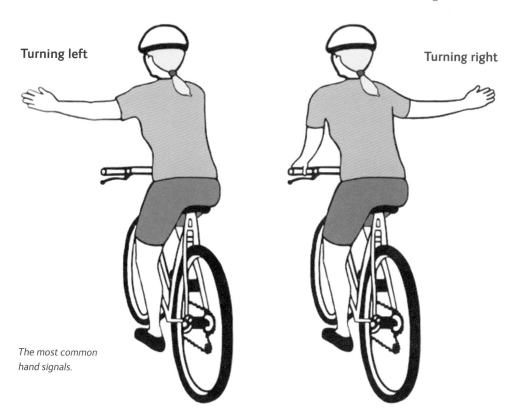

Turning left

Turning right

The most common hand signals.

The Half Signal

This is not an official signal but it's one I frequently use. If I have taken a position in the centre of a lane and am getting ready to move back to the inside of the lane, I will indicate with my arm pointing at an angle, about halfway to the full position. This lets the driver behind me know that I am moving back to the kerb. This can also be used when you are moving rapidly between lanes.

Correct Posture

Good cycling posture is important because of the stresses the body experiences, particularly from jolting, which can affect your back, shoulders, neck and wrists. A good cycling posture allows the muscles to absorb shocks.

1. To save knee and hip pain, make sure that the seat is at the right height for you. When you are riding, your leg should be slightly bent at the knee. To set your saddle height for this, sit squarely on the saddle, propping yourself against a wall for support. Don't lean over with your hip and don't slide forward. Your heel should be able to just touch the pedal at its lowest point, six o'clock. If your leg is bent or you can't reach the pedal, adjust the height of the seat.

2. The handlebar should be level with, or not more than an inch lower, than the seat. You can adjust the height of the handlebars if you need to. The important thing is that when you hold the grips, the backs of your hands extend at much the same angle as your forearms. If your wrists are bent, particularly down, then you can injure them, as jolts and shocks will not travel up the arm to be absorbed by your muscles.

3. With the seat and handlebar now set properly, when you ride, keep your back arched out slightly rather than curved in as you would if sitting in a chair. This allows the back to absorb shocks better, thus preventing the development of back pain or injury. On road bikes, where the rider leans forward more, this curving out of the back may be more noticeable than on a recreational bike where you are more upright, but nonetheless, the back should still be relaxed and slightly curved outwards.

4. Keep your elbows slightly bent rather than locked. Doing this means that the muscles in the arms act as shock absorbers.

5. Push your shoulders forward so that your chest muscles can help support your upper body, and keep your upper back slightly rounded.

Adjusting to the New Posture

Sustaining this posture will not be easy at first. You can develop it by doing short rides of just a few miles to begin with and gradually extending the distance. If you are cycling regularly, perhaps to work each day, just do the first few kilometres in the new posture and, if you start to feel discomfort, relax back into your old posture. In time you will be able to sustain the new posture for longer periods.

Top Tip

If you have any regular aches and pains after cycling, check the height and angle of the seat, and the height of the handlebars. A very slight adjustment may be all you need to make.

Riding in a Straight Line

A surprising number of cyclists actually wobble or weave slightly. To ride in a straight line, use the kerb as your guide, keeping about half a metre away from it. For all riders the possibility of wobbling increases when looking back, or when signalling to turn. Developing a good cycling posture and pedalling properly will help you to reduce this. A good place to practise is an empty car park where you can use the parking-bay lines as a guide.

Top Tip

If you want to cycle but feel nervous on the roads, you can take a cycling proficiency course to develop your skills and confidence.

The Right Approach

Riding a bike well involves not only the physical techniques, but also an attitude of mind. There are many riders for whom fear is a strong factor in how they ride. Such riders might avoid changing gear or hug the kerb too closely. This is neither fun nor safe. There is a better way to ride. A safe rider is a confident rider, and this book will help you gain the knowledge and skill to fill you with confidence.

THE HAZARDS OF CYCLING

Despite the perceived vulnerability of a cyclist, research has shown that the risks are relatively small compared to other forms of transport and activity, but these risks can be reduced even more through a full awareness of the potential hazards and how to deal with them.

The Fearsome Four

Although there are hundreds of potential dangers, the sheer number of which are enough to cause a measure of anxiety in any rider no matter how experienced, it is possible to organize them all into just four more manageable areas:

- The bicycle
- The cyclist
- Other road users
- Environmental factors

The Bicycle

The hazards presented by the bicycle are essentially due to mechanical failure. Regular cleaning, lubrication, checks and maintenance will considerably reduce such risks. The following is a simple list of checks that you should make on a regular basis:

Top Tip

Taking a short course in bicycle maintenance will give you the ability to detect and repair problems before they become accidents.

- **Brake levers:** Stand next to your bicycle with your hands on the handlebars and push the bike forward as you apply both brakes firmly. The bicycle should stop before the levers have moved halfway to the handlebars.

- **Brake pad wear:** Check that the brake pads are not too worn. Most brake pads have grooves in them. Change the pads, a pair at a time, when they are so worn down that the grooves have almost vanished.

Clean brake pads: Inspect the pads for grease or to see if they are shiny. Rub the surface of the pad with sandpaper if they appear shiny or greasy. If you cannot remove grease thoroughly, replace both pads before riding.

Brake pad damage: Examine the pads for debris embedded in them. Remove any you find and inspect the pad for any damage that could interfere with braking. If you find one damaged, replace the pair.

Brake mounts: Pull and push the brake mountings. Tighten them if there is any looseness.

Brake alignment: Make sure that the brake pads are properly aligned. Pull the levers and look at the pads on the rim. There should be no overlap above or below.

Brake cables: Check that brake cables are secured tightly at the brakes and not frayed at the ends. If loose, tighten the pinch bolt and if frayed, trim the end of the cable with cable cutters and fit a cable end cap.

Wheel rims: Examine these for dirt and grease. Wipe them clean with soapy water if they are dirty. You can use degreaser or citrus-based solvent, but make sure not to get any on the tyres or brake pads. Ideally remove the wheel and the tyre before cleaning the rims with solvents.

Handlebars: Try to rotate the handlebars forwards. If there is any movement, tighten the bolts that secure the handlebars to the stem.

The headset: Whilst holding the handlebars with the brakes on, rock the bike back and forth. If you can feel any looseness or hear a clunking sound, the headset (see page 149) is probably loose. See www.flametreepublishing.com/extras for further info on how to check and adjust headsets.

Wheel security: In turn, hold each wheel by the rim and try to move it from side to side. If there is more movement than a few millimetres, check that the securing nuts or quick-release are tight. If after tightening there is still movement in the wheel, the bearings will need to be checked by a mechanic.

Wheel alignment: Look down the forks from above to see if the wheel is centred between them. If not, you will need to re-centre the wheel before riding.

Gears: A chain that comes off whilst you are riding, or gets caught in the derailleur, can cause you to be thrown. Once a week run through your full set of gears to make sure that the chain doesn't come off. If it does, you will need to adjust the limit screws or have them adjusted for you.

Tyre pressure: Pressure begins to diminish, albeit slowly, from the moment you inflate your tyres, so pump them back up to their ideal pressure every week.

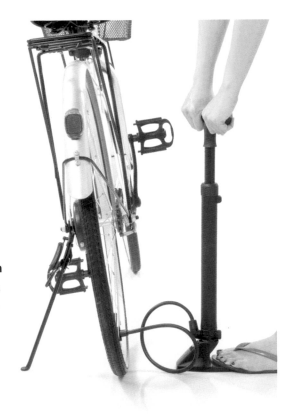

Top Tip

Buy a floor pump with a pressure gauge as it is easier to inflate your tyres with than a hand pump, and also means you can get the pressure exactly right.

Tyres and tubes: Remove anything that has penetrated your tyres and allow 10 minutes or so to see if they are deflating. Don't cycle on deflated tyres, as it will damage your rims. Small cuts in the tyre can be mended by drizzling superglue or wetsuit repair glue into them.

Tyre tread: Every so often take note of the wear on your tread. Good tread is very important as it provides grip on the road. Worn tyre tread will cause you to lose control of the bike, which will skid on wet roads or when you brake hard.

Lights: If you are going out at night, in low light or in poor visibility, make sure that your lights are working properly, are securely attached and pointing in the right direction. Light-mounting brackets often work themselves loose.

Reflectors: Many accidents for cyclists occur when they are hit from the side at a junction, turning or roundabout. Make sure you have reflectors on your wheels and give them a wipe with a cloth every week.

Luggage: If carrying any weight on the bike, make sure it is secured properly in the basket, panniers or on the rack. If using panniers, balance the weight as well as possible on either side.

Racks and baskets: Check that these are attached properly and the securing nuts are tight.

Mudguards: Check that these are secured properly and not catching on your tyres.

The Cyclist

Having control over the functioning of the bike is easier than having full control over ourselves. Getting into the habit of having the right equipment with you, and being physically and mentally prepared, will significantly reduce the risks.

The Basics

The greater your skills, knowledge of the road and state of preparedness, the safer you will be. Skills were covered in the previous chapter and knowledge of the road will come later in this one. The following are some of the basic things that you can do to increase your safety by being prepared:

Warm up: After completing your bicycle checks do a warm up. For more about warming up, see page 121 in the chapter on *Health, Leisure & Sport*.

Top Tip

You can warm up at the start of your ride by pedalling rapidly (high cadence) in a low (easy) gear. After a few minutes you can shift into higher gears and your normal cadence.

Be seen: Make sure you are wearing something bright even in normal daylight. A high-visibility vest, tabard or gilet is ideal for daylight, but for night riding make sure to have something containing reflective material like 3M Scotchlite.

Clothing: Make sure you have the right clothing for the conditions. These could include rainwear, sunglasses, gloves and a hat. Clothing should also be comfortable without being so loose that it might tangle in the bicycle.

Helmet: If you wear one make sure it is not damaged and is secured properly.

Trouser clips: Reflective ones are best. Either way, you don't want to mess up your trousers by having them tangle in the chain, nor do you want to be thrown from the bicycle.

Medical ID: If you have any medical conditions, are of a particular blood group, or are on medication, carry this information in your wallet or purse.

First-aid kit: A basic one for dealing with cuts and scrapes is enough. It would include an antiseptic for direct application and suitable dressings. Remember that if you do fall and scrape along the ground, you may have a large surface area to cover, so gauze pads and surgical tape are best.

Top Tip

If you are planning to commute to work or do your shopping by bicycle, but feel concerned by the traffic, do a test ride on a Sunday when the road is quieter.

Water: If you are cycling for more than a short commute or shopping trip, take some water with you. Symptoms can become noticeable after losing just two per cent of your normal water volume. It can lead to cramps, dizziness and visual distortion, amongst other things.

Sun protection: On sunny days put sunscreen on before going out and take some with you if you are going to cycle for longer than an hour.

Route planning: Be clear about your route before setting off. Panicking about a missed turn or suddenly stopping to check directions sets you up for a possible accident.

Other Road Users

Although you cannot know what someone else is going to do, there are situations that arise where the potential for an accident is higher so, knowing what these situations are, you can at least be prepared for them.

Vehicles

The following list, from a study of cycling accidents, details the most serious types of collisions between cyclists and vehicles. The list is in order of frequency, with the first being the most common:

- Exiting a driveway in front of an oncoming vehicle.
- Turning in front of a passing vehicle.
- The motorist was overtaking the cyclist, cause of the accident unclear.
- Riding on the wrong side of the road.
- Riding on the wrong side of the road and then turning across traffic.
- The motorist was overtaking the cyclist and failed to see him or her.
- The cyclist lost control and swerved into the path of the vehicle.
- The cyclist made a normal right turn (left for those cycling in a right-hand-drive country) but ignored oncoming traffic.
- The motorist lost control of the car and struck the cyclist.

Reducing the Risks

Apart from the third and ninth causes, all of the others are within your control to a greater or lesser extent. Let's look at how you can deal with these situations:

- **Joining traffic:** Look carefully before pulling out of a driveway or joining traffic.

- **Turning and overtaking:** Always look behind you before making any turns or overtaking, and give clear signals.

- **The right side:** Always ride on the correct side of the road and never against traffic on a one-way street.

- **Be seen:** Wearing high-visibility clothing and using good lights at night will help drivers to see you.

- **Maintaining control:** Situations where you might lose control of the bicycle will be reduced by keeping it serviced and developing good riding skills.

Top Tip

In any situation where you feel that the conditions are dangerous for you, simply dismount and push your bicycle until you are in a safer situation.

Vigilance

Even in those situations where the driver loses control, or hits the cyclist whilst overtaking, can be reduced by being attentive to the road. Listen to traffic coming from behind and check over your shoulder frequently, especially when approaching turns on your side of the road, parked vehicles, other cyclists, drains, potholes or other obstructions.

Large Vehicles

The height of lorries and buses means that there is a point where the driver can't see you in his or her side mirrors. For this reason it is best not to undertake such vehicles or, if you must, be very careful. Undertaking means to pass the vehicle on the inside. If such a vehicle suddenly starts to turn on your side of the road, you could be crushed against railings or dragged under the rear wheels. Passengers on buses may also step off ahead of the bus stop.

Motorcyclists

It is best to treat motorcycles in the same way as you would cars. The main concern for a cyclist in regard to motorcycles is their considerable speed combined with their low visibility compared to cars. Sometimes motorcycles travel on the inside of a line of stationary vehicles rather than outside, so keep your eyes and ears open.

Pedestrians

Pedestrians have a habit of stepping on to the road without looking. Being aware that they do this can be enough to prevent an accident. Moments before a pedestrian steps off the kerb, he or she will be moving towards the kerb, so if you are alert you will see it coming. That's where a bell is useful.

Pedestrians also have a habit of stepping on to crossings even though the lights are against them. If you have a bell, ring it. Remeber, too, for your and their safety that it is illegal and dangerous to cycle on pavements and walkways unless designated for cyclists.

Other Cyclists

The main situation to be aware of in regard to other cyclists is overtaking. This could be you overtaking a cyclist or vice versa. We will look at this in more detail towards the end of the chapter in the section, 'On The Road' (see page 89).

Environmental Factors

For the sake of convenience these can be divided into two types: natural and man-made. Volcanoes, floods and earthquakes aside, the natural hazards are basically weather, whilst the man-made ones are various obstacles and conditions that can impact on you as a cyclist.

Weather

One of the great beauties of cycling is being in the natural elements. However, this can be a disadvantage too. Prolonged exposure to certain weather conditions, extremes of weather and extreme changes in weather can be disastrous for cyclists.

Heat

It doesn't get much better than a day's cycling on a lovely summer's day. However, being exposed to the sun can cause two main problems:

- **Sunburn:** Being in a fixed riding position means that you don't get to hide certain parts of your body from the sun. Forearms, thighs, calves, neck, head, face and ears can all burn very quickly. Use a good sunscreen and for longer rides wearing UV-resistant clothing would be a good idea.

- **Dehydration:** Dehydration can begin to affect you very quickly. Symptoms include dizziness, visual impairment and muscle cramps, all of which can seriously affect your ability to ride safely. Drink plenty of water before a cycle ride on a hot day and take water with you.

Sunlight

Sunlight shining directly into the eyes, very bright conditions or reflections off vehicles or other objects can impair your vision at any time of year. Sunglasses are a must. Ideally, get wraparound or goggle-type sunglasses, as light can get in behind ordinary sunglasses and reflect back into your eyes.

Cold

Apart from making you feel very uncomfortable if you are not dressed properly, the cold can affect your ability to change gear and, most importantly, brake, due to your hands being stiff. For cold weather dress appropriately and wear good gloves that are not so chunky they inhibit your movements.

Wind

Unless it is at your back the wind is no friend of the cyclist. Side winds are the worst and if very strong can buffet you into the road or the kerb. The best thing to do if you feel that the wind is impairing your control of the bicycle is to dismount and walk.

Mist and Fog

As with night cycling and low light conditions, make sure you can be seen by wearing high-visibility clothing and carrying good lights on your bike.

Rain

Apart from making you wet and uncomfortable if you haven't brought waterproof clothing, the rain can pose several hazards:

- **Wet surfaces:** Rain on the road reduces traction between your wheels and the road surface. This in turn can make you more likely to skid. Firstly, ride with care in wet conditions. Secondly, don't brake when taking corners or roundabouts, as braking causes you to lose even more traction. Slow down before the bend if you are going too fast. Avoid manhole covers, tramlines and other metal objects, which become particularly slippery. Rely more on the rear brake.

- **Driving rain:** This wind and rain combination is rare, unpleasant and there isn't too much you can do about it apart from squint, keep riding and hope for the best or play safe and walk instead.

- **Puddles:** Puddles are nature's way of saying, 'There's a dip here', so avoid them. The dip could be deeper than your bicycle can cope with. If it's a big puddle and you have to go through it, do so very slowly. It might help to stand on the pedals for extra balance and cushioning if you do hit a pothole.

- **Reflection:** I mentioned this when talking about sunlight, but will mention it again because it is important. Just because it's a rainy day don't forget to take your sunglasses. It may happen that a little while later the sun peeps through and you find yourself dazzled by the reflection off the wet road.

- **Leaves:** Dry leaves are not a problem but wet ones can be, especially if they have been left to mulch. Ride around them if you can or, if you have to go over them, avoid braking. If you need to brake, use the back brakes more than the front, and don't lock either wheel but brake gently.

Snow and Ice

Even though they are different entities for the cyclist, I have put these two together because they often happen at the same time. Contrary to what you might think, snow isn't really a problem for cyclists. Ice is, however, so don't cycle if you expect icy conditions. Here are some tips for riding in snow that may also help if you encounter ice.

- **Chunky tyres:** Don't try riding in snow without some. You could do it but you are increasing the risk factor, especially if you encounter any ice.

- **Get a grip:** Keep both hands on the handlebars and keep most of your weight back on the seat.

- **Easy gear:** Riding in an easier gear will give you more control as you won't be pushing the pedals so hard.

- **Tyre pressure:** Lower the pressure in your tyres a little as this gives more traction.

- **Metal objects:** As with wet roads, avoid manhole covers, tramlines and other metal objects.

- **Body weight:** Don't lean into corners and bends as much as you would normally. Take them slowly.

- **Braking:** As with wet conditions, don't brake on bends. Brake on the straight. Avoid using the front brake and don't lock the wheel. Brake gently.

- **Skidding:** Should the rear wheel start to slide, continue pedalling slowly but firmly if you can, but there's no harm in putting a foot down to save a fall.

Man-made Hazards

These are predominantly objects or conditions in your path that can cause you to fall or swerve. That may sound obvious but at least it breaks the solution down to the same essential response: take note of what is in front of you, even if you cycle the same route every day.

- **Potholes:** These are an obvious hazard to a cyclist so keep an eye out for them, especially after a bad winter.

- **Road furniture:** Drains, tramlines, rail tracks and manhole covers are potential problems when wet, and they are often sunken so can have the same impact as potholes. Ride around them whenever you can, but it is better to ride over them slowly than to swerve out suddenly.

- **Litter and debris:** Pieces of paper are rarely a problem, but some litter can be large or awkward, such as glass bottles, broken glass, broken umbrellas or plastic bags. Shredded tyres, broken exhaust pipes and other vehicle flotsam can also turn up in your path.

- **Protruding items:** These are rare but it can happen that objects stick out into the road, such as the fronts of pushchairs, people's luggage or other items left leaning across railings and safety barriers.

- **Water sprays:** Water that is sprayed on to dry roads, especially dusty roads, by garden sprinklers, cafés and shops, people washing their cars and so on can cause you to skid.

- **Oil:** Bus stops, delivery points and the approaches to busy junctions and traffic lights, where cars often queue, are common places where oil will drip. When wet these areas can be very slippery. If you ride through any obvious oil, wipe the tyres and wheel rims as soon after as possible. If you need to brake on such surfaces, use the back brake more than the front, and don't lock either wheel but brake gently.

- **Gravel and grit:** As with oil, leaves and wet conditions, loose surface material can cause you to skid, so it is best to use the rear brake more than the front.

ON THE ROAD

So, now you are almost prepared for your cycling adventures. You have your bicycle, the necessary equipment and accessories, you know your riding technique and are aware of the various hazards that can threaten your safety. The final things to learn are your road skills: the business of actually riding in traffic and dealing with turnings, junctions, roundabouts, road position, overtaking and so on.

Important Note

In this section I will write about directions a lot. As I am British, those directions are for British roads, which are left-hand drive. Therefore, references to left and right should be reversed for any country that is right-hand drive.

Riding Straight Ahead

Although this may seem the simplest of things to do, there are some points you need to bear in mind.

Vehicles Turning

To avoid being hit by a vehicle turning left, don't undertake an indicating vehicle at a junction. Undertaking is where you pass on the inside of vehicles that are moving slower than you or are stationary. Sometimes a car may overtake you and then, with little or no warning, turn left. This is where being visible is important, having good brakes and also allowing space between you and the kerb.

Vehicles Pulling Out

When approaching a side road to your left, be vigilant for vehicles pulling out that haven't seen you. If you see a driver at such a junction, no doubt watching traffic for an opportunity to pull out, try to catch their eye so that you know you have been seen. Otherwise, check behind and, if you have the opportunity, move further out into the road.

Left-turn Lanes

If you intend to ride straight ahead but you are in a left-turn-only lane, then move out into the main lane and treat the dividing line between the left-only lane and the straight-ahead lane as if it were the kerb.

Junctions

If you intend to go straight ahead at a junction or roundabout, then move into the middle of the lane about 50 metres before the junction. I will explain later, in the section on 'Overtaking' (see page 87), what to do if there is a queue of traffic waiting at the junction. Hold the centre position until you are actually on the junction and then move back to the left-hand side of the lane. The reason for this is to prevent a vehicle that is turning left from turning into you, which is possible if you are on the inside of the lane.

Top Tip

Be confident about taking control of a lane by moving into the middle of it. It will considerably reduce the risk of many common accidents.

Making Turns

Left turns are relatively straightforward. Right turns can be more complicated because, apart from crossing the lane you are in, and possibly more than one lane, you also have to cross oncoming traffic (it is the opposite in right-hand drive countries, of course!).

Making a Left Turn

It's best if you can take the middle of the lane even for a left turn. You only need do this a short distance before the turning, about 25 metres. This will give you more room to lean into the turn but, most importantly, it will prevent a vehicle coming behind you, that also intends to turn, from hitting you.

Making a Right Turn

About 75 to 100 metres before reaching your turning, check behind, indicate and move to the centre of the lane, then, if there is no oncoming traffic, make your turn. If there is more than one lane, you will need to make your move sooner.

Oncoming Traffic

If there is oncoming traffic preventing you from making an immediate right turn, then when you reach the turning point, stop in the centre of the road – not the centre of the lane – so cars that are going straight ahead can pass on your inside. Only complete the turn when there is plenty of distance between you and oncoming vehicles. This will allow time for recovery should any mishaps occur, like your foot slipping off the pedal as you start off.

Roundabouts

These are probably the most challenging aspect of cycling. Even small, innocent-looking roundabouts can be dangerous. The only time I have ever been hit by a car and knocked off my bike was on a small roundabout when traffic was light. Fortunately no damage was done, but had I been one second faster it could have been serious.

Top Tip

If you are in any doubt about a roundabout, junction or intersection, dismount and go the pedestrian way.

Exiting Left

Once on the roundabout, if you are turning left, treat it as any other left turn, except be very alert for vehicles coming from your right that also intend to use that exit. Some drivers do not indicate clearly on roundabouts but you can often judge their intentions by looking at their faces.

Going Straight Ahead

As with a junction, once you have moved on to the roundabout, begin to move back to the left of the lane. Keep an eye out for vehicles already on the roundabout coming up behind you. Also keep an eye on the drivers wanting to join the roundabout to make sure they have seen you. Wave if you think they haven't.

Exiting Right (Smaller Roundabouts)

These have just one or two approach lanes, and one or two lanes on the actual roundabout. Take the middle of the lane if it is one approach lane, or the middle of the right lane if there are two, giving a clear right-turn signal as you do. On the roundabout keep to the centre of the lane and signal again so that drivers entering the roundabout from the opposite side can clearly see where you are going. As you round the top of the roundabout make a left signal, to show that you are exiting, and cut across the lane or lanes towards your exit.

Exiting Right (Larger Roundabouts)

These have one or two approach lanes, rarely three, but will have three lanes on the actual roundabout. Do as for smaller roundabouts on the approach, but once on the roundabout, instead of taking the centre of the right-hand lane, use the middle lane or, if traffic is moving fast, stick to the dividing line between the second and third lanes, allowing cars to pass on either side. Be extra vigilant for cars coming from behind, as well as those entering the roundabout from the left and directly opposite the side you entered.

Overtaking

There are various overtaking scenarios, including overtaking bicycles, being overtaken by bicycles and undertaking, which is where you pass on the inside of vehicles.

Overtaking Motor Vehicles

This is only likely to happen when traffic is moving very slowly or at a standstill, usually because of a junction ahead. Ideally, it is best to move out from the kerb and overtake the line of traffic. To do this, check behind you a good distance before you have reached the back of the queue, indicate and move across to the other side of the lane. That is easy enough. The trickier part is getting back, or making a left turn further ahead.

- **Traffic starts:** If the traffic starts to move as you are overtaking, you will have time to make eye contact with a friendly driver and signal that you wish to come back across the lane in front of them. If this is a junction and you are going straight ahead, stay in the centre of the lane until you have passed the left turning, then move back to your normal road position, checking for cyclists coming up the inside.

- **Static traffic:** Cycle all the way to the front of the queue on the outside, dropping to your lower, start-off gear as you approach the stop line. Sometimes there are advanced stop lines for cyclists to use. If not, stop and take your starting position next to the lead vehicle. You will probably start more slowly than the cars, so don't feel you have to race ahead. Start as normal, keep your line and as you get to a reasonable speed, look back inside, indicate that you wish to come back across the lane, catch a friendly eye and make your move. Watch out for cyclists coming up the inside.

- **Turning ahead:** You may wish to turn left at the junction ahead so you will therefore have to move back across the traffic. To do this, aim to move back into the lane much earlier than if going straight ahead. If the traffic is stopped but likely to move off soon, then stop about seven cars back from the front, and indicate to the driver behind that you intend to move into the lane. Once you are let in, stay in the middle of the lane whilst indicating, until you make your turn.

Undertaking

You could undertake a line of slow moving or stationary vehicles, but take great care in case a passenger opens a door, people get off a bus or a vehicle turns left and cuts you up.

Overtaking Another Cyclist

As you approach another cyclist, check behind you for vehicles, indicate and, when there is a gap, overtake, allowing plenty of room for the other cyclist. If the road is very busy, it is best to fall in behind the other cyclist, giving them plenty of room in front.

Top Tip

Stop lights are a good place to overtake another cyclist. Just pull up alongside them and ask if you can go ahead when the lights change.

Being Overtaken by a Cyclist

When looking over your shoulder don't just look for motor vehicles, look for bicycles too. If another cyclist is approaching, continue to ride as normal and simply allow them to overtake you as and when he or she is ready. Don't try to help them by stopping or slowing down. Before they overtake, check the road ahead for any hazards like drains, potholes or parked vehicles. If you see any, then indicate to the cyclist behind, and any other vehicles, that you are pulling out.

Overtaking Parked Vehicles

Look back, signal and move out when there is a gap, as you would when overtaking anything else. However, make sure to have the space of an open car door between you and the parked vehicles. If this means that you take the centre of the lane then do so. Better the grumblings of an irritated driver than colliding with an opening car door.

Cycle Lanes

Designated cycle lanes can offer a false sense of security because, as they take you off the main road, they take you out of a driver's consideration. This is fine for the duration of the lane, but cycle lanes frequently rejoin the road, especially at junctions, so take great care in such situations.

Narrow Roads

Near where I live is a wide, busy road that narrows considerably as it bridges a river. The majority of cyclists cross this bridge by riding on the pedestrian walkway. Apart from being illegal and unsafe, it is very unpleasant for the pedestrians. The solution to such narrow stretches is to hold your position and not move closer to the kerb. If cars get too close for comfort, then take the middle of the lane if it is safe to do so, and make the traffic go at your pace. Alternatively, dismount and walk.

Riding in Groups

Riding in close proximity to other cyclists takes practice. The lead rider sets the pace and is responsible for communicating to the group any hazards ahead. This is usually done by voice and the message is passed back through the group. Generally, you can cycle in pairs but single file is polite on narrow stretches. Avoid making any sudden movements and always communicate with the group before you need to slow down or stop. If you become separated at junctions or on hills, find a safe place to regroup.

CHECKLIST

⚙ **Clean start and stop:** Practise pushing off so that you experience less wobbling. Remember to look behind you and change down to your start-up gear before stopping. Remember to use your front brake more than your rear brake unless the road surface is slippery.

⚙ **Pedalling:** Practise the 'oval clock' method to get more power into your pedalling and use a high cadence supported by smooth gear changes.

⚙ **Signals:** Give clear signals in good time to alert other road users to your intentions.

⚙ **Posture:** Adjust your saddle if it is too high or too low and develop a good cycling posture to save yourself aches, pains and injuries.

⚙ **The bicycle:** Conduct regular checks of your bicycle and make sure you lubricate the moving parts on a regular basis.

⚙ **Be seen:** Wear high-visibility clothing and make sure you have good lights. Assert your space rather than cower in the gutter.

⚙ **Weather and hazards:** Be prepared for changes in the weather. Understand the likely hazards you might encounter and how to deal with them.

⚙ **Vigilance:** Get into the habit of regularly checking over your shoulder for other cyclists as well as cars. Expect the unexpected, be attentive to the environment and try to anticipate potential accident situations.

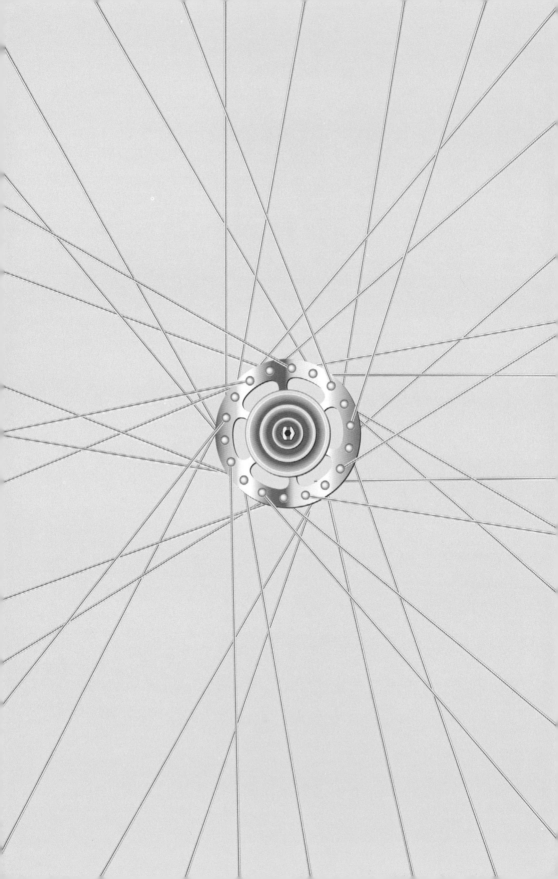

EVERYDAY CYCLING

THE CYCLING REVOLUTION

More and more people are waking up to the fact that cycling is a credible means of transport in its own right, one that has many advantages over the car and other forms of transport. This chapter looks at the benefits and practicalities of cycling for everyday use, for commuting and shopping and how that can work even if you have children.

Eye Opener

You may have noticed cyclists overtaking queues of traffic, day after day, during the rush hour. Perhaps you have seen a neighbour leisurely returning from a shopping trip on a bicycle loaded with the weekly shop and perhaps even a child. It could make one wonder whether cycling might actually be a better way to travel. It is and there are many reasons why.

Time

For most city commutes, cycling is quicker than any other form of transport. In the UK around 4 million people drive less than three miles to work. An average cyclist would do that in 15 minutes. Given the build-up of traffic during the school run, cycling instead of driving would also be as quick if not quicker, and more enjoyable.

Door-to-door

Cyclists do not have to walk to bus stops, train stations, change buses or trains, or find parking spaces and then walk from those to the office, shop or school.

Predictability

The door-to-door advantage of cycling, combined with a cyclist's ability to get through traffic and route around hold-ups, makes commute times predictable to within a few minutes.

Savings

Cycling is the cheapest form of transport after walking, and the difference in costs for a cyclist and a car owner are immense, literally thousands of pounds every year.

Health

Cycling is one of the best forms of exercise a person can do, and it can also be used to improve fitness, so it's a means of transport and an exercise routine all in one. As nearly a quarter of primary school children in the UK are considered to be overweight, it is a perfect way to address that problem.

Child Friendly

Children are generally happier as passengers on bicycles than they are in cars, whilst older children with their own bicycles benefit more from cycling than being transported in a car, bus or train. Aside from the health benefits, a recent US study showed that physical activity has a positive effect on performance in school tests.

Load Bearing

Bicycles are excellent packhorses. With the right attachments you can easily load them up with the weekly shopping, children and even pets.

Top Tip

Ask your school or local authority if they encourage cycling to school and if they offer any support. Many do.

PREPARATION

One of the beauties of cycling is the ease of simply being able to get on your bicycle and go. However, before achieving that easy freedom, there are some things to consider and prepare so that you will have an easier, more comfortable and more enjoyable experience.

Feasibility Study

The following list covers just about everything you would need to consider before taking up cycling on a regular basis:

- **Equipment:** Do you have chain oil and the basic tools for essential adjustments? Do you have lights, a bicycle lock, safety wear, first-aid kit, suitable clothing, a puncture-repair kit and a means to carry luggage, ideally not on your back?

- **Health and fitness:** Do you have any health conditions that might be affected by cycling? If your journey is likely to be a long one, are you confident of your ability to do it at your current level of fitness?

- **Storage:** Do you have access to secure storage for your bicycle at home and at your journey's end, preferably somewhere dry?

Top Tip

If you take up regular cycling, then buy a basket or pannier rack where you can easily store your laptop, work clothes, waterproof clothes, puncture-repair kit and still have room for some shopping.

⚙ **Facilities:** Do you think you might need access to special facilities at your destination for washing, changing and storing a change of clothes? If so, are they available? If they are not available, is there a suitable alternative or can you ask your employer to provide something?

⚙ **Safety:** Have you read and understood the two previous chapters on cycling technique and safety?

⚙ **Public transport:** If you plan to take your bicycle on public transport for part of your journey, have you checked with the transport provider about any rules or requirements that they may have or if there are charges for your bicycle? Some buses in the US have bike racks on the front for you to store your bike while you ride.

Buses in some countries allow you to transport your bike in externally mounted racks.

⚙ **Security:** Do you have insurance and is your bicycle registered with the police? Do you have the details of your bicycle, including the frame number, serial numbers of expensive parts and do you have a photograph of the bicycle, preferably a digital one?

Breakdowns: If you don't have an instant puncture-repair kit, do you have a traditional one, and do you know how to use it? Can you replace a chain that has slipped off the sprockets? Find out how to fix a puncture on pages 157–58 and how to put your chain back on on page 172.

 Route plan: Have you investigated all the possible routes to your destination? There may be some that are shorter, safer, prettier or all three. Have you noted potential areas of hazard and planned how you will deal with them?

Further Thoughts

Of the points regarding feasibility some may be obvious, irrelevant, self-explanatory, covered in more detail elsewhere in this book, or easily solved now that you are aware of them. However, there is one on the list that I will cover in more detail, as it is not covered elsewhere in this book and is very important to every cyclist: security.

Security and Theft

Unfortunately, the theft of bicycles and bicycle parts is an all too common crime. Over 2 million bicycles are stolen every year in Europe and the same number in the US. There are ways to reduce the risk and, in the event of a theft, things to do to recover your bicycle or its cost.

Secure Locks

None is proof against theft but some are better than others. Here are the main options (see also page 48):

⚙ **Chain**. A heavy-duty motorcycle chain lock is useful to leave attached to your regular bike stand.

⚙ **Shackle:** The U-shaped lock is widely available, with the better ones generally being more expensive. A disadvantage of these locks is that they only secure one wheel and the frame. I therefore recommend that you use it in conjunction with a cable lock.

⚙ **Cable:** A cable lock comprising many braided strands of wire is better than one with fewer strands.

Combining Locks

Thieves want to be as quick as possible, so having to break two locks is off-putting, not to mention the fact that each requires a separate, bulky tool.

Secure Locking

Always lock your bicycle to something that is as solid and immobile as possible, preferably a metal object fixed to the ground or a wall. Many bicycles are stolen from sheds and garages, so lock your bicycle to something secure even when it is inside. Thieves will remove an unlocked wheel, so make sure that both wheels are locked to the frame.

Locking the Bicycle

Position the shackle lock around the rear wheel and the frame tube. A smaller lock will fill the space the lock covers, making it harder for the thief to insert and work a tool. Turn the lock mechanism towards the ground or a wall and keep the whole lock off the ground. Use the cable lock to secure the front wheel to the frame and also to the bicycle stand, railings, lamppost or similar. With a long cable you can also secure your saddle.

Top Tip

You can personalize your bicycle with a respray and add your own custom stickers. These are called 'decals' and can be bought quite cheaply from many companies online.

Secure Place

If you can store your bicycle indoors, then so much the better.

If you have to lock your bicycle outside, find somewhere in public view or with CCTV surveillance.

Unattractive Bikes

A bicycle that is cheap, personalized with a home paint job, or scuffed, scratched and shabby, is less attractive to thieves as the sale price is low. As your bicycle is for work or shopping then you don't need anything too fancy. Top-of-the-range bikes tend to be for high-performance sports.

Securing Parts

Thieves will take parts from a bicycle, hence the need to secure both wheels. If you have a seat with a quick release, then you can remove it each time, replace the quick release with a bolt or run your cable lock through it, the frame and the front wheel. Remove any bags, clip-on lights or the like.

Expensive Parts

Other parts like gears and brakes cannot be easily removed, but they do sometimes get stolen if they are top-of-the-range and your bicycle has been left in a secluded place. An extreme option is to use paint or a rotary tool to erase the brand name, but it won't be pretty. Bear in mind that it will lower the resale value for you just as for any would-be thief. Make a note of the serial numbers of parts to give to the police should they be stolen.

Marking and Registering

Contact your local police about having your bike security marked. It is usually free, certainly inexpensive and could well get your bicycle back if it is stolen. The police should also take the frame number of the bike and your contact details. Once marked you should get a sticker that states the bicycle is marked and registered. Display this on the frame where it is easy to see. There are also national registries like www.bikeregister.com for the UK or www.nationalbikeregistry.com in the USA.

Bicycle Details

Take a photograph of your bicycle and get some close-ups of any distinguishing features or marks like scratches. Make a written note of the make, model, colour and frame number. You will find the frame number stamped on the underside of the frame between the pedals (the bottom bracket), or some older bikes have it on the seatpost clamp. You may find that other parts also have serial numbers, so it is worth noting those down.

Theft

In the event that your bicycle is stolen, it is important that you follow these steps. It is believed that up to 50 per cent of bicycle theft goes unreported because people assume that the police can't do anything about it. They can and so can you.

⚙ **Tell the police:** Tell the police immediately and provide them with details of your bicycle, even if it is already registered. If you have not registered it, you will need your receipt as proof of ownership. It is worth carrying a description, including any distinguishing features like obvious scratches, plus a photo of your bicycle, and your contact details with you. Tell the police precisely where the bicycle was stolen from and if there are any CCTV cameras in the vicinity.

⚙ **Sound the alert:** Post a message on your local bicycle forums with a description of the bike and upload a photograph if you can. I know of one case where a woman did this and, immediately after posting, two forum members saw a similar bike on an auction website and alerted her by private message. It was indeed her bicycle and was recovered by the police.

⚙ **Become a detective:** Go online and look for bicycles and parts of your type being sold on auction sites. Thieves with a little intelligence will make changes, so look carefully and look at the seller's record. What is their feedback and what kind of things are they selling? If you see a bicycle or frame that you suspect is yours, alert the police. This is why keeping a record of the frame number and parts' serial numbers is so important.
The police can go and look. Check the classified adverts in the local paper too.

Insurance

Given that a bike is stolen every minute, insuring your bicycle would be a wise thing to do. As insurance can also cover for accidents, personal injury and claims made against you, it is worth the price of the premium. Check if your bicycle is already covered on your home insurance. There will be all manner of provisions, so check the details. It might only be covered when it is on the property or if you have a certain type of lock. It might not cover accessories.

COMMUTING AND SHOPPING TIPS

Now that you have everything in place, you can jump on your bicycle and away you go, whether that's to the office or to the shops. Before you do though, here are some extra tips that you might find useful.

Commuting

- **Pannier rack:** I have always used a pannier rack even if I haven't always used panniers. They are excellent for carrying things like clothes, books, files and laptops. Many children say they can't cycle to school because they have too many books.

- **Clothing:** Unless it is very hot, if you cycle at a steady pace then you shouldn't need a change of clothes. However, I recommend that you cycle in casual clothes and leave smart clothing at work, or carry them on your rack wrapped in a strong plastic bag or in a pannier.

- **Mudguards:** If you are going to wear your smart work clothes or a school uniform, make sure to have mudguards fitted, otherwise your clothes may be soiled by dirt thrown up by the wheels in wet weather.

- **Shoes:** If you prefer to cycle in your work shoes rather than leave them at work, or carry them on the rack, you can protect them from rain and street dirt with cycle overshoes.

⚙ **Money:** Make sure you have some money with you in case your bicycle is stolen or you have a breakdown. At least you will be able to get home by public transport.

Shopping

⚙ **Packing:** Place heavier items lower down and lighter ones higher up, and try to balance the weight on either side of the bike.

⚙ **Carriers:** Use panniers, a basket or a trailer for your shopping. Whatever you do, don't hang carrier bags on the ends of handlebars as it will play havoc with your steering, and don't carry much on your back as it could easily cause you harm.

Top Tip

For shopping or commuting don't waste money on fancy panniers. You don't need waterproof ones as long as anything you want to keep dry is wrapped in a plastic bag first.

⚙ **Tyres:** Make sure your tyres are inflated to the recommended level, as it will be easier to cycle when you are carrying a load.

⚙ **Riding:** The balance, pace and handling of your bicycle will be very different on your way home compared to your outward journey. This contrast can catch you out. Tour cyclists who carry all their equipment can take a few days to get used to it. Ride home with care and expect a wobble or two until you have adjusted.

⚙ **Bungee cords:** In the event that you buy a little more than you had intended, take a couple of bungee cords with you to secure the extra to your luggage rack.

CHILDREN AND CYCLING

Cycling is great for children in all sorts of ways, whether as passengers on your bicycle going to school or the shops, travelling independently on their own bicycles, or simply enjoying cycling for sport and recreation. It's all good, wholesome fun. In this section we will look at the basics of getting children involved in cycling and cover the key safety issues.

Early Start

You can involve children in cycling from the very beginning of their lives. A newborn baby can be transported in a bicycle trailer and an older baby can be carried in a child seat attached to your bicycle. There are also tandem bikes, trailer bikes and tow bars that offer a range of other ways to involve smaller children.

Child Trailers

Trailers for children are becoming more popular and, should you wish to try before you buy, they are often

Top Tip

Getting your children used to cycling from an early age will make it second nature for them. They will learn a great deal about how to cycle properly just from being with you.

available at bicycle hire centres. They will have a safety harness, at least one seat, possibly two, a rain cover, windows and other features, depending on the make. Most can fold easily, helping with storage and transportation. They are attached to your bicycle with a bar. Weight capacity is around 45 kg (100 lb). If you want to carry a newborn baby, make sure that the trailer you buy has the necessary fittings.

Child Seats

For a baby that is able to support its own head you can mount a child seat in front of you, between the saddle and handlebars, or behind you.

- **Front seats:** Front-fitting seats are less common than rear-fitting ones. You might feel happier having your baby in front, though not many offer support for the shoulders and head, which are useful to have if your baby falls asleep. Some riders manage this by supporting their baby's head with a hand, but that means less control of the bicycle so isn't recommended. The weight limit of these seats is around 15 kg (34 lb).

- **Rear seats:** These are much more common than front seats, offering a wider variety of features, such as adjustable headrests, reclining backs, rain covers and storage compartments. The weight capacity ranges from around 18 kg (40 lb) for basic seats, to 22 kg (48 lb)

for better-quality ones. Seats that attach to a rear pannier rack will generally be sturdier.

Trailer Bikes

Also known as a 'tag-a-long', this is effectively the back half of a child's bicycle, the front section being a frame that attaches to the rear of your bicycle, so there is no front wheel or steering. They are for children aged between four and nine. The child can pedal or just freewheel. There are also tandem versions so two children can be towed, although you might want to encourage them to help with the pedalling!

Tow Bars

Similar to a trailer bike is a tow bar, although you will need to check the fittings, weight and suitability for your child's bicycle.
The tow bar attaches to the child's bicycle, converting it into a trailer bike. When attached, the bar lifts the front wheel of the child's bicycle off the ground so they cannot steer, but they can pedal if they wish. The weight limit of these bars is around 30kg (65 lb) including the child and the bicycle.

Tandems

It is possible to get tandems with a lower seat for children. Bike Friday make several folding versions, including the Family Tandem Traveller with an adjustable seatpost that will fit anyone from 1 m to 2 m (3¼ ft to 6½ ft), and the Tandem Triple which will take two adults and one child, or one adult and two children.

Top Tip

Keep cycling trips with very small children short, especially if you are carrying them in a seat on your bicycle, as boredom will probably lead to wriggling which will make balance and steering harder.

Children's Bicycles

In the chapter *Choosing a Bicycle* on pages 16–21, there is a review of the different sizes of children's bicycles. Here, I will just say that the earliest a child is likely to be able to ride with you, on his or her own bicycle, will be aged five. Even then, you and your child may feel it is safer or more convenient to use a trailer, bike trailer, tow bar or tandem for journeys together. Your child can still have his or her own bicycle for use in a safe cycling area for play and developing good riding skills.

Learning to Ride

In terms of the very basic skills of being able to balance and pedal without crashing into something, the vast majority of children learn to do this in their own good time. However, you can help to make it a quicker and easier process for them. What makes it difficult for them is the combination of pedalling and trying to balance at the same time, as the act of pedalling moves the weight from side to side. Here's how to make it easier for them:

 No pedals: Start training without pedals, and remove any stabilizers. You can buy trainer bicycles without pedals in the smallest wheel size for children, or remove the pedals from a standard bicycle. Make sure that the seat is low enough so your child can sit with his or her feet flat on the ground. It will only take a handful of practice sessions, on a gentle slope, for your child to develop good balance.

With pedals: Once your child has learnt to balance well, he or she can then start to learn with pedals. As starting is the difficult part of maintaining balance, give your child a gentle push so that he or she achieves the momentum necessary for maintaining balance without having to pedal. Once moving and balanced, they can try the pedals. They will only manage a few revolutions before having to put a foot down but, with a few practice sessions, they will soon get the hang of it.

Top Tip

When teaching your child to ride, use a gentle grassy slope. You can also tape insulation foam around the bicycle tubes to protect your child from knocks and bangs should they fall.

Developing Skills

Once the child can balance and pedal after a push start, teach them how to start off on their own. You can read about this in the *Safe Cycling* chapter on pages 60–61. Once this is mastered, introduce some more skills like how to brake properly, sit properly, signal and so on. When the child is older it will be well worth sending them on a cycling proficiency course.

Independent Cycling

Children love to cycle, but not that many do. Apart from a few niggles about carrying books or wearing skirts, most children are happy to cycle to school, or would be if they had the opportunity. However, this isn't available to them as only 20 per cent of children in the UK cycle to school, the majority discouraged by parents who fear for their safety.

The Danger Myth – Safe Cycling for Children

As I have shown earlier in this chapter and elsewhere in the book, cycling is not only much safer than people think, but as the British Medical Association has said, the benefits outweigh the risks. That said, child cyclists are injured and killed on the roads every year, albeit fewer than children as pedestrians and car passengers. If you teach your children to cycle properly and prepare them for the road, the risk is minimal. The following should be read in conjunction with the previous chapter on safe cycling.

Equipment

A prime reason for accidents involving child cyclists is that motorists don't see the child. Once an accident occurs, the main cause of fatality and serious injury is trauma to the head. For your child's safety make sure he or she uses the following:

⚙ **Clothing:** Bright clothing should always be worn and preferably with reflective material like 3M Scotchlite. This can be integrated into cycle clothing and bags, or you can buy it as a self-adhesive roll and attach it to items the child will wear when cycling.

⚙ **Flag:** You can buy safety flags, usually sold for recumbent cyclists, that easily attach to the back of the child's bicycle. These are important as a child on a bicycle can be low to the ground and missed by motorists.

⚙ **Reflectors:** Fit four reflectors, front and rear and both sides. The side reflectors attach to the spokes of the wheels.

⚙ **Lights:** There should be two, one at the front and one at the rear, and they should be available to the child at any time, including during the day, if he or she is cycling anywhere near a road. Ideally, fit dynamo lights. The child can simply ride with them on all the time.

⚙ **Helmet:** There are many, but they are not all of equal quality. The best have Snell certification. To find out more visit the website www.smf.org.

Top Tip

Give your child regular lessons on safe cycling in a traffic-free area such as an empty car park before they ever cycle on the road. Reward them for the skills and knowledge they have learnt.

The Bicycle

Don't buy a cheap bike, especially one with plastic wheels. Buy a good bicycle from a bicycle store and make sure that it is maintained properly. You can do this yourself, ideally involving your child, or have it serviced regularly by a bicycle mechanic. Perform safety checks with your child before going out on a ride. You can read about these in the *Safe Cycling* chapter on pages 70–73.

Top Tip

Before your child undertakes a solo journey, cycle the route with them several times, taking note of any potential dangers, good places to cross the road, sections where it would be better to cycle on the pavement, and so on.

On the Road

Once you have read the *Safe Cycling* chapter, apply the knowledge and understanding to children with the following exceptions and additions:

- **Driveway:** A very high proportion of accidents involving children occur when they ride out of their driveway on to the road. Don't let them do it. Walk the bicycle out and on to the pavement or road and then mount the bicycle when the road is clear.

- **Pavement:** Let children, up to teenage, cycle on the pavement where roads are busy. Police officers will make an exception for them. It is best for the child to ride on the outer edge of the pavement as cars may pull out of driveways. Make sure your child is aware of this possibility and is on the alert.

- **Junctions:** Rather than attempt to negotiate these, including roundabouts, it will be safer for the child to use a pedestrian crossing.

CHECKLIST

⚙ **Equipment:** Make sure you have the necessary equipment for maintaining your bicycle and keeping yourself comfortable and dry.

⚙ **Luggage:** Think about how you will carry your possessions. A rear pannier rack is a very worthwhile investment.

⚙ **Locks:** Have you got a lock or, preferably, two locks that will secure your wheels to the frame and the bicycle to a solid object?

⚙ **Bike details:** Write down the frame number for your bicycle, serial numbers for any parts and take a photograph of your bicycle to have with you when you cycle and store on your computer.

⚙ **Make it official:** Register your bicycle with the police or a national bicycle registry.

⚙ **Insurance:** Investigate getting some bicycle insurance. With good locks and your bicycle registered with the police, you will get a better deal.

⚙ **Involving the kids:** If you want to involve your children in cycling, visit a good bike shop to find out what equipment and bicycles are available. Take details of your existing bicycle to see what equipment is best suited to it.

⚙ **Safety:** Teaching your child to ride a bicycle is more than just about balancing and pedalling. Teach them all the skills and knowledge of safe cycling.

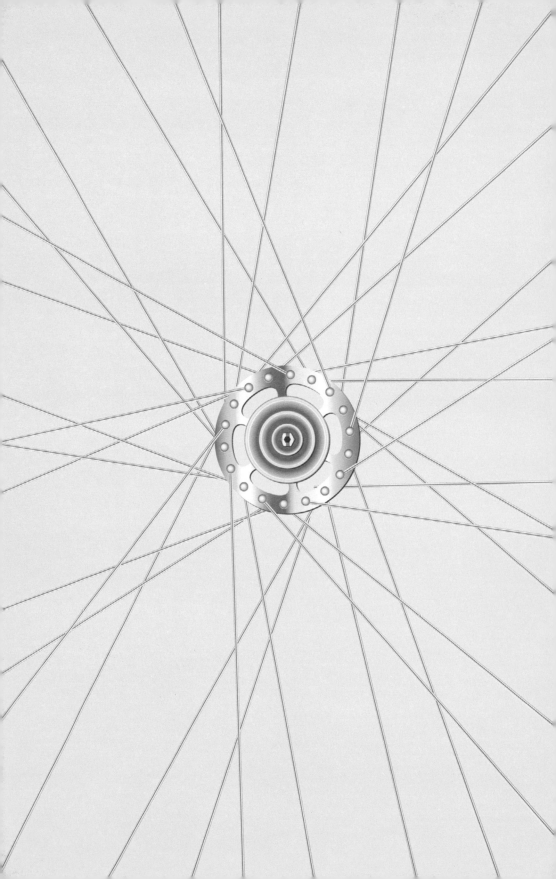

HEALTH, LEISURE & SPORT

LOOKING GOOD, FEELING GOOD

Cycling is one of the best ways to develop and maintain excellent health and fitness. Easy cycling for 30 minutes a day is enough to help maintain a basic state of good health, whilst higher levels of fitness and stamina can be achieved through cycling as part of a training programme or sport.

The Road to Health

Cycling is an excellent way to achieve the recommended 30 minutes of moderate exercise, five days a week. Doing this will protect you against a wide range of illnesses, whilst at the same time getting you from A to B. Apart from improving your health, it will also boost your fitness levels. It's said that a person who cycles every day has the same level of fitness as someone 10 years younger.

The Evidence

There is a great deal of solid evidence to support the claims made for cycling's benefit to your health. The following are just a few examples:

⚙ **Mortality rates:** A Danish study tracked the health of 17,265 men and 13,375 women between the ages of 20 and 93 over a period of 14 years. Of those, 15,000 cycled regularly, 7,000 of them cycling to work. The results showed that 'even after adjustment for other risk factors, including leisure time physical activity, those who did not cycle to work experienced a 39 per cent higher mortality rate than those who did'.

⚙ **Heart attacks:** A similar study in the UK monitored the health of 9,000 civil servants between the ages of 45 and 64 over a period of nine years. It was found that those who cycled at least 25 miles a week experienced less than half the number of heart attacks compared to those who took no physical exercise.

⚙ **CVD:** Over a 10-year period, a Finnish study looked at the effects of activity and non-activity on the health of 19,000 people aged between 25 and 74. One group only performed light activity, whilst the second group performed 4 hours of moderate activity a week such as cycling. It was found that being obese or inactive increased the risk of cardiovascular disease (CVD) by 35 to 70 per cent.

The Effect on Your Body

Cycling offers many health benefits for your whole body and your mind as well:

⚙ **Weight loss:** Being a physical exercise, cycling is an obvious way to lose weight. Just half an hour of cycling a day can burn off 10 kg (22 lb) of fat in a year. Cycling is especially good for those who are very overweight as it allows them to exercise without straining their joints. Maintaining a healthy diet as well as cycling will be even more effective.

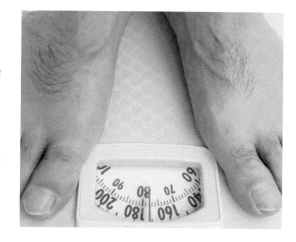

⚙ **Respiratory system:** Moderate physical exercise like cycling benefits the lungs, increasing their ability to absorb oxygen. This in turn benefits cell metabolism for the release and use of energy throughout the body.

Top Tip

Did you know that short, moderate cycle rides four times a week for just six weeks will boost your aerobic fitness by at least 11 per cent?

⚙ **Immune system:** Infections are amongst the most common health problems even if most are not serious. Fighting off such infections requires a healthy immune system. Moderate exercise has been found to cause immune cells to circulate more quickly through the body, making you better able to neutralize bacteria and viruses. Although the immune system returns to normal a few hours after exercise ends, regular exercise does appear to make these changes longer lasting.

⚙ **Cardiovascular system:** Cycling is excellent exercise for the heart and circulation, helping the heart to become much more efficient. The process of burning up fat also has a positive impact on your cholesterol. Cycling will cause your normal pulse rate to slow down which, in turn, can help reduce blood pressure.

⚙ **Muscles**: These need to be used regularly to keep them in optimum condition. In just one week of inactivity you can lose up to half of your muscle strength and flexibility. When cycling, you are not just using the leg muscles but those of the buttocks, abdomen, back, chest, neck and arms.

⚙ **The skeletal system:** With the correct posture, cycling helps to strengthen the skeletal system and enhance skeletal mobility. Cycling can help to nourish the intervertebral discs, aiding their development, strengthening the muscles of the back and promoting the stability of the vertebrae.

⚙ **Joint protection:** The particular movements of pedalling help to increase the flow of nutrients to the cartilage of the ankles, knees and hips, thus strengthening these joints. Furthermore, for those who already suffer from joint problems, cycling offers one of the least stressful ways of strengthening the joints and gaining the general benefits of exercise without damaging them further.

⚙ **Stamina:** This refers to the body's ability to cope with tiredness and fatigue. It can be developed through aerobic exercise such as cycling.

- **Diabetes:** A 12-year study of 20,000 people in Finland found that those who cycled for more than 30 minutes a day reduced the risk of developing diabetes by 40 per cent.

- **Cancers:** Regular exercise has been shown to reduce the risks of cancer. Furthermore, research has shown that if you cycle, the risk of contracting bowel cancer could be reduced.

Top Tip

Someone weighing 63 kg (140 lb) will burn around 200 calories during a 30-minute, moderate cycle. Balance your diet to take account of this extra activity, and drink more water.

- **Mental stress:** Even though it is a form of exercise, cycling is very relaxing, as effortless as walking and with less strain on the joints. Add to this the fact that exercise releases endorphins, the body's happy chemicals, and you have a wonderful means of de-stressing. So, after a hard day at work, cycling home can be an ideal way to unwind.

- **Depression:** As cycling has a positive effect on how you feel, it can be very helpful in easing the misery of depression. This is enhanced further if you take your cycle rides in some beautiful countryside.

- **Wellbeing:** The overall combination of improved health and fitness, reduced stress and the sheer pleasure and exhilaration offered by cycling is guaranteed to help you look and feel great.

Before You Go

Before attempting any cycling for fitness you need to start with moderate cycling so your body can become accustomed to it, and before starting with moderate cycling there are things that you need to do to prevent injury or accident. After all, what is the point in setting out to improve your health and fitness only to harm yourself in the process? Familiarize yourself with the points in the *Safe Cycling* chapter on pages 58–91, and how to warm up and cool down as discussed on the following pages, before taking up cycling regularly.

Warming Up

Warming up before exercise is important because your muscles will not be very flexible if they are cold. Cold muscles are more likely to be torn or pulled, unlike warm muscles, which have a greater range of stretch and contraction. Your warm-up exercises should take no more than a few minutes, but don't rush them.

Warm-up Exercises

There are many types of warm-up exercise you can do, but the main thing is to get the body warmed up. Dynamic (moving) stretches are considered better than static ones. I also do a set of loosening-up exercises for the joints, although they're not essential. If you don't know how to do stretches properly, it is best to have someone who knows how to show you. After stretching, continue the warm-up on your bicycle by pedalling for a few minutes at a higher cadence than you would normally use and in a lower, easy gear.

Top Tip

Stretching should be done slowly and in an easy motion. Don't push a stretch beyond the comfort level. Exhale when you go into a stretch and inhale as you come out of a stretch.

Cooling Down

You may have noticed that after exercising you can feel light-headed and later your muscles become stiff. Performing a cool-down helps to prevent this, allowing your blood pressure and heart rate to gradually slow down, clearing out the by-products of exercise like lactic acid and carbon dioxide, and helping to reduce the level of adrenalin in your blood. Depending on the intensity of the exercise, cool-downs can take from three to 10 minutes. You will know when you are done as your pulse rate will be close to normal.

Cool-down Exercises

A few minutes before the end of your ride, slow down and pedal in a lower gear, giving your legs an easier ride. With the pressure off, but your legs still working a little, you will gradually cool down. As soon as you have finished the ride do some gentle stretching for a couple of minutes and, if you have been doing a fitness-oriented ride, have a hot shower or bath. This will help to prevent the muscles from stiffening up.

Moderate Cycling Plan

If you are thinking of taking up cycling after a lengthy absence, as with any physical activity, it is not a good idea to try to do too much straight away. The following steps will help you and your body to become accustomed to the activity so that you will be able to comfortably cycle for 30 minutes a day, five days a week.

Flexibility

These steps allow a month to build up to the target, but if you are very unfit, it could take longer. Don't rush it. You'll get there. If you are already quite fit, you can move through the programme more quickly by adjusting it to suit your level.

Top Tip

If you experience any persistent aches or pains after cycling, and your posture is good, make a tiny adjustment to your seat height and then see how it feels next time.

☼ **Check first:** If you have any health conditions, first ask your doctor about the recommended levels of initial exertion.

☼ **Good to go:** Even if you are cleared to ride for more than 20 minutes a day, I suggest that you begin with no more than 15. Cycle one day and rest the next day. Do this for three rides over six days.

☼ **Technique:** I recommend that for your first three rides you find a traffic-free place, like a cycle route or a large, empty car park, and spend the 15 minutes developing your cycling skills. In regard to your health, the important ones to learn are your posture, pedalling and gear-changing technique. For safety, get used to the brakes.

☼ **Getting underway:** After your first three rides, you can then cycle for 20 minutes on two consecutive days before taking a rest day. Then cycle for 25 minutes for two days, take a rest day, then 30 minutes for two days, then rest. If at any point it feels like a strain, ease off. Rest an extra day and then try again until you are comfortable cycling for that amount of time.

☼ **Gearing up:** Once you are comfortable with cycling for 30 minutes for two days out of three, you can increase the frequency to three consecutive days, rest a day, and then cycle for 30 minutes on four consecutive days, rest a day and then do five consecutive days for 30 minutes each day.

CYCLING FOR FITNESS

Aerobic exercise raises your rate of respiration and your heart rate, circulating oxygen and nutrients faster and more efficiently. This leads to the development of stamina, which is your body's ability to be more active for longer before becoming fatigued. Cycling for high levels of fitness demands a little more effort than for everyday cycling.

Nutrition

This is essential for cycling generally, but especially so for training, sports and activity cycling. The bottom line is that you need energy for physical activity and your body only stores limited amounts of it.

Balanced Diet

Your doctor or local health centre will have information on diet, as will many health websites. Balanced diets are usually based on the assumption that you do 30 minutes of moderate exercise a day, so you will want to increase your carbohydrate and protein intake whilst doing any fitness training.

Top Tip

If cycling for several hours or more in a day, take a little more food with you than you think you might need. It's your reserve tank of fuel.

Calorie Counting

Whether undertaking moderate or fitness cycling, you will burn calories for energy. A person weighing 70 kg (150 lb) will burn around 270 calories during 30 minutes of moderate cycling. For 30 minutes of fitness cycling this will increase to around 350 calories. For longer periods of cycling the number of calories burned increases significantly:

- **Two hours: 1,085 kcal**
- **Four hours: 2,170 kcal**
- **Six hours: 3,255 kcal**
- **Eight hours: 4,340 kcal**

Fuelling Up

It is essential that your body has enough calories to meet the requirements, just as you would make sure you had put fuel in the car. You can easily find information from your local health centre or online about the calorific values of different foods. Keep it healthy though!

- **Last supper:** Eat a good meal the night before a long ride. Fill up on carbohydrates like pasta, potatoes and rice.

- **Breakfast boost:** Eat a good breakfast an hour or so before setting off. This could be a couple of pieces of fruit and some cereal, eggs and bread.

- **Top-ups:** Take a few snacks with you like bananas, cake or energy bars. If you are comfortable eating as you ride, have a nibble every half hour, otherwise stop every two hours to eat something.

- **One more:** Your muscles will benefit from a snack within 15 minutes of completing your ride. A slice of cake, banana or the like will be enough.

Water

Water is vital for numerous critical bodily functions, hence the reason that we cannot survive for very long without it. It is essential to the process of energy release, amongst other important things. Key functions that water plays a role in are:

⚙ **Digestion:** Water is essential for the digestion and absorption of food.

⚙ **Temperature:** It helps to regulate and maintain our body temperature, especially as a coolant through perspiration.

⚙ **Cushioning:** Fluid in the joints and tissues aids in their movement and protection from shocks.

⚙ **Circulation:** Blood depends on water for its fluidity, which in turn aids the transportation of oxygen and nutrients to all the cells of the body.

⚙ **Metabolism:** Water is essential for metabolism: the processes of energy release and cell development.

⚙ **Lymph:** Water aids the lymph system to move toxins and infections away from the cells, ready for excretion.

⚙ **Excretion:** Water plays a crucial role in the elimination of various toxic elements and other waste products from the body.

Drink Up

It is recommended that a person drink at least eight glasses of water a day to maintain optimum hydration. This is all the more important when undertaking exercise, as you lose water through sweating. That said, be wary of drinking too much. During exercise, in moderate temperatures, the body can cope with 500 to 750 ml (17 to 25 fl oz) every hour.

⚙ **Before:** Drink at least eight glasses of water the day before a long ride. In the morning, before your ride, sip your way through four glasses of water, ideally spread out from waking to 20 minutes before setting off.

⚙ **During:** Drink a few mouthfuls of water every 10 minutes during the ride. Don't wait to get thirsty, as this indicates that you are already dehydrated. In warm weather, aim to consume at least half a litre (1 pint) every 45 minutes to an hour. For longer rides, make sure there are places on your route where you can refill your bottles. The colour of your urine is generally a good indicator of hydration levels. The darker it is, the more dehydrated you are.

⚙ **After:** Drink a glass of water every hour once you have finished your ride. If you are likely to be cycling on consecutive days, it is very important that you maintain hydration. If you don't, a few days in you will start to feel fatigued very quickly.

Top Tip

Hydration packs are very useful for fitness training and long rides as they allow you to cycle and drink more safely than having to reach for a water bottle.

Fitness Cycling Plan

There are many different ways that you can use cycling to develop your strength and stamina. The following plan would be good for anybody, but would be very useful for cyclists who are not particularly fit but who need to train for a cycle touring holiday, a charity cycle or who simply want to get fitter without having to join a gym. If you haven't cycled for a long time, unless you are very fit, you will first need to follow the moderate cycling plan described earlier.

Structure

This programme runs for a month with five days of half-hour routines, followed by a sixth day of longer rides. This should bring you to a level of fitness suitable for a touring holiday or long-distance cycling event. Obviously it will depend on your level of fitness to begin with, but if you cycle regularly, it is doable. If for any reason you find it a struggle, or you experience any adverse effects, stop and rest. If necessary take a few rest days instead of the one prescribed.

Location

It would be best if you could find somewhere to do the half-hour exercises that allows you to keep cycling without having to stop frequently for traffic lights or junctions. Have a look online or ask at your local tourist office to see if there are any cycle routes near you. If you don't have somewhere particular to do the exercises, or are short of spare time, you could work the exercises into your daily commute.

A Note on Breathing

How you breathe is important during exercise, especially vigorous exercise, so get into the habit of breathing deeply, in a regular pattern, inhaling through your nose and exhaling through your mouth.

The Plan

⚙ **Day 1**: After your usual five-minute low-gear, high-cadence warm-up, ride in a low cadence for 10 minutes in one gear higher than you would normally use for that terrain. After the 10 minutes is up, shift down to an easier gear and ride at a normal cadence for five minutes. After that, do another five minutes at a low cadence and higher gear before cooling down for the last five minutes. The cool-down is a slower cadence and easy gear.

⚙ **Day 2**: As you complete your five-minute warm-up, select the appropriate gear for the terrain, but pedal at a higher cadence than normal and keep going for 20 minutes. This is a good exercise for learning how to pace yourself. Five minutes before the end of the ride, start your cool-down.

⚙ **Day 3**: After your usual five-minute warm-up, switch to a higher gear and normal cadence for five minutes, then drop to the lower gear again and pedal at high cadence for five minutes. Keep alternating between a high and normal cadence every five minutes. If you are doing it right, you should be breathing hard during the high-cadence sections. If not, then you will have to pedal faster. After 25 minutes, begin the cool-down.

⚙ **Day 4**: After your warm-up using a high cadence and low gear, shift to one gear higher than you would normally use for the terrain for five minutes, then drop to a

Top Tip

It is worth investing in a cycle bag that attaches to your handlebars or the frame. This way you can access snacks as you ride and carry other useful items like sunglasses, sunscreen and a puncture-repair kit.

lower gear and increase the cadence for five minutes. Alternate between these until five minutes before the end of your ride, to allow for the cool-down.

⚙ **Day 5**: Warm up for five minutes then put on a fast burst of speed for 20 seconds, then slow down for 20, then back to the fast burst again, then the slow and so on for five minutes. For the next five minutes, ride as normal to recover before going back to the fast, 20-second bursts for another five minutes. Keep this up until your normal cool-down time.

⚙ **Day 6**: Enjoy a normal yet steady cycle for two hours. Eat a good meal the night before and a good breakfast about an hour before you set off and make sure to keep yourself properly hydrated.

⚙ **Day 7**: Rest, relax and maybe do a little bicycle maintenance.

⚙ **Week 2**: Repeat the training except, on day six, ride for four hours with a 10-minute break after two hours. Cool down before breaks and warm up after starting again. Make sure to eat a meal and drink plenty of water before setting off and take water with you. Eat a snack in your break like an energy bar, fruit cake or banana.

⚙ **Week 3**: Repeat the training except, on day six, ride for six hours. You can take a short break after two hours followed by a longer one for lunch after four hours.

⚙ **Week 4**: Repeat the training except, on day six, ride for eight hours. You can take a short break after two and six hours, and a longer one for some lunch after four hours.

Top Tip

Before going on a cycle tour, do a practice run over a long weekend, especially if you are going to be carrying luggage, and don't ride for more than six hours each day.

CYCLING FOR PLEASURE

There is much more to cycling than a cheap, fun and green way to get to work or the shops. You can go a step further into the world of cycling through a number of cycling activities and sports that serve a broad range of tastes and experiences. Beyond day trips in your local area there are several great ways to combine cycling and pleasure without becoming an athlete or getting covered in mud: riding local and national cycle routes, trail riding, taking your bicycle on holiday, touring and mixed-terrain touring.

Cycle Routes and Trails

More and more cycle routes are being created all the time. Some routes are entirely traffic-free, whilst others incorporate sections on public highways. They are usually created by national and local government agencies, often in conjunction with cycling organizations. Such routes make for excellent family days out.

History and Scenery

The best cycle routes take in sites of historic interest or natural beauty, and provide picnic spots and information points. Many follow disused railway lines, canal towpaths or riverbanks, whilst

others have been developed in woodland, around lakes or through national parks. They are usually well signposted and maps can be obtained either online or from tourist offices and libraries.

Trails

Some routes consist of dirt or gravel tracks. A mountain bike is perfectly suited for such trails, but not essential as many bikes can cope with them, particularly trekking hybrids with their knobbly tyres. These bicycles are generally cheaper than mountain bikes but do the job well enough. However, it is best not to take them on to any truly challenging terrain, for which only a mountain bike is suitable. If riding trails, make sure you have your tools, puncture-repair kit, food and water, a first-aid kit and your phone.

Taking Your Bicycle on Holiday

By taking your bicycle, or hiring one at your destination, you can enjoy relaxing rides to local attractions, or nip to the shops or beach. Taking your own bicycle is easier than you might think, and you will have the benefits of mobility, familiarity of handling and saving on the rental fee.

Transporting Your Bicycle

There are numerous types of rack for transporting bicycles on cars – use bungee cords to hold it in a stable position to avoid damage. Bicycles can also be transported on trains, ships and planes, but it is wise to check with the transport companies beforehand. Folding bicycles are ideal as they can be stored in the boot of a car and taken on public transport more easily than a full-size bicycle – you can buy hard-cover bicycle boxes to protect them. That said, if you are planning to take a folding bike by plane, it is still wise to check with the airline beforehand.

Safety and Theft

Taking your bicycle on holiday should not cause any extra risk, but check with your bicycle, home, car and travel insurers what cover you have for your bicycle whilst on holiday and make sure to lock your bicycle in the safest place possible. See pages 98–102 in the *Everyday Cycling* chapter for advice on security.

Top Tip

If carrying your bicycle on your car, lock it to the rack, not just to keep it from falling off, but to prevent someone from stealing it if you stop somewhere.

Cycle Touring

This is a perfect way to enjoy the great outdoors and experience a range of spectacular scenery, at a pace that allows you to take it all in, whilst getting fitter at the same time.

Fitness Level

If you've never done it, I recommend you train in advance using the fitness programme in the previous section. At the very least, you should take a few trips close to home, carrying a similar amount of equipment as you expect to on your tour. This way you can gauge the distance you can comfortably do in a day. Several days of consecutive cycling can take a toll on your energy levels, so make sure to include some rest days into your itinerary.

What Kind of Bicycle

For road touring there is a classic style of bicycle that is described on pages 32–33 in the *Choosing a Bicycle* chapter. You can still use other bikes though, as long as they have low gears, a luggage rack, a comfortable seat and a sturdy frame. Visit www.flametreepublishing.com/extras for further advice on carrying your luggage and what equipment and toolkit you will need to take.

Top Tip

Gaffer tape is a handy extra to take with you on a tour for on-the-spot repairs. It is designed to peel off more easily than duct tape so is great as a temporary fix.

Mixed-terrain Touring (MTT)

This is also known as 'rough stuff' or 'rough riding' and includes variations on the theme such as alpine touring, adventure touring and snow biking. The names say it all, describing forms of cycling that involve riding on a variety of terrain and surfaces. Visit www.flametreepublishing.com /extras for further info on MTT.

Freestyle BMX

Freestyle BMX is a generic term for five different disciplines – Street, Park, Vert, Trails and Flatland. They tend to be most popular with younger riders. Visit www.flametree publishing.com/extras for further info on Freestyle BMX.

SPORTS CYCLING

There are a surprising number of cycling sports, several of them Olympic disciplines. They involve a broad range of skills and appeal to an equally broad range of people. Aside from being a way to get fit, cycling for sport is a great way to meet like-minded people through membership of a club or association and competing in events. Here I give a brief overview of the different sports out there. If you want to learn a little more, visit www.flametreepublishing.com/extras.

BMX Racing

Now an Olympic sport, Bicycle Motor Cross (BMX) is most popular with younger riders, although it is also a great family activity, as parents who don't ride will often get involved as coaches, mechanics, organizers and supporters. Races involve riders of similar age or ability competing around a 300- to 400-metre track with humps, bumps and banked corners called 'berms'.

Top Tip

Before spending money on expensive equipment, join your local club first as they usually loan equipment to beginners and, as a club member, you may be able to get a discount at local bike stores.

Cycle Speedway

Appealing to male and female, young and old, cycle speedway involves racing on outdoor dirt tracks, 65 to 90 metres in length. There are separate matches for Under 8, Under 10, Under 13, Under 16, Under 19, Open and Over 40. Races are sprints taking less than a minute and, given that physical contact is legal and the bicycles do not have brakes, this makes for a very intense and exciting sport.

Cyclo-cross

Cyclo-cross, also known as CX, CCX and cyclo-X, is a very easy sport to get involved in and is becoming increasingly popular. It involves racing in laps around a short course of 1.5 to 3 km (1 to 2 miles). Courses can include grass, wooded tracks and sand, and they contain obstacles such as steep banks, steps, barriers and pits that force riders to dismount and carry their bikes. Courses are designed so that a rider will carry his or her bike for about 10 per cent of the course.

Top Tip

Sports cycling associations will usually publish a diary of competitions online, so you can go along to see the sport in action, and meet and talk to organizers and riders about getting involved.

Mountain-bike (MTB) Racing

Various disciplines of MTB racing have evolved in recent decades. Five of the most popular are downhill, four-cross, cross-country, marathon and enduro. Their names are self-explanatory, with four-cross (4X) involving four riders competing on a short, downhill course featuring a variety of BMX-style obstacles.

Road Racing

The Tour de France has probably made road racing the most recognized of all cycling sports. It has a long history, being an event at the first modern Olympic Games held in 1896. Road racing requires considerable fitness and tactical ability. Teams will draw on the strengths of individual members to maximize their advantage in changing terrain. Typically, races are massed-start with up to 200 competitors. They take place on roads or Tarmac

Top Tip

Although equipment is expensive for most cycle sports, it is unlikely that you will need to buy it all in one go. Instead, buy what you can afford each month to build up your kit over time.

circuits, with distances ranging from 20 km (12 miles) for junior competitors to 40 to 100 km (25 to 60 miles) for adults. For top riders there are races of 200 km (120 miles) or more, with tours lasting days or even weeks.

Track Racing

Races are on specially built, banked tracks, often called velodromes. These vary in design and length. Olympic-standard tracks are 250 metres, indoor and made of wood. Outdoor tracks are concrete or Tarmac and often longer. There are two main types of track race: sprint and endurance.

CHECKLIST

⚙ **Health check:** Consult your doctor if you have any conditions before taking up cycling.

⚙ **Nutrition:** Make sure that you are getting enough calories for any fitness training that you undertake, and that you keep your energy levels up with regular snacks whilst riding.

⚙ **Water:** Make sure to drink plenty of water if you are cycling for half an hour or more. You'll need at least 500 ml (1 pint) for every hour of cycling.

⚙ **Starting:** Ease back into cycling after a long absence by following the moderate cycling programme.

⚙ **Fitness training:** Prepare for cycle touring or long-distance rides with the fitness programme provided.

⚙ **Insurance:** If getting involved in sport or recreational cycling, check that you have full insurance cover for the activity.

⚙ **Routes and trails:** Go online to find your local, regional and national cycle routes, or visit the tourist office to ask about cycle routes and any free maps.

⚙ **Public transport:** Before taking your bicycle on public transport check the provider's regulations.

⚙ **Clubs:** Contact your regional or national sport cycling association to find out about local clubs and events.

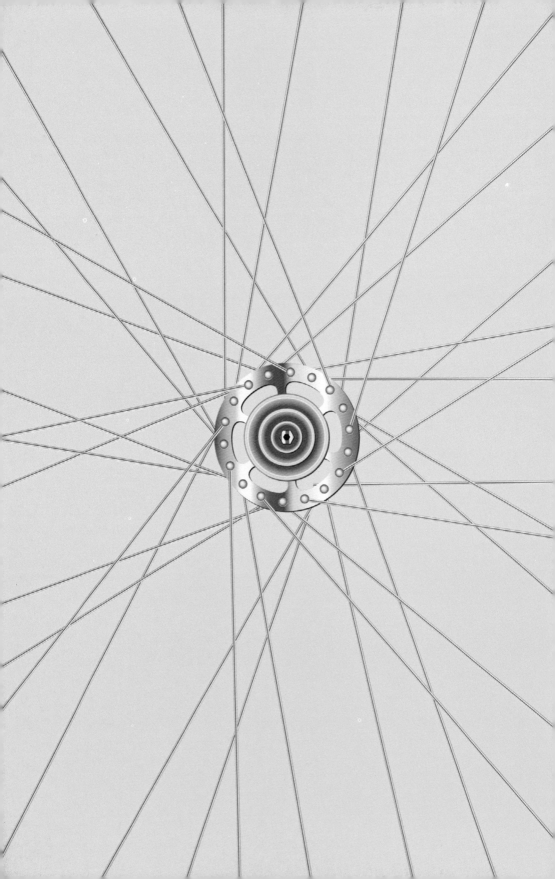

BICYCLE MAINTENANCE

DO IT YOURSELF

Bicycles are easier to maintain and repair than you might think. Spending an hour on a regular basis maintaining your bicycle will help preserve its life and prevent breakdowns and accidents. Here I detail some basic tools you should find useful – the investment in tools will save repair costs in the long run. In the following sections I cover some of the basic tasks you will benefit from being able to do. We cover some slightly more fiddly tasks at www.flametreepublishing.com/extras.

Basic Tools

The following list of tools and supplies covers only those items that you are most likely to need in basic bicycle maintenance, rather than specialized tools that will be mentioned separately where appropriate. Bicycle multitools can be very useful and inexpensive. Most of the jobs featured in this chapter were done using a Park MTB-3 Rescue Tool (see opposite).

Set of Allen Keys (2–8 mm)

These are also known as hex keys and hex wrenches. They are used on screws and bolts with a hexagonal-shaped socket in the head.

Set of Spanners

Also called wrenches, you may need one or more ranging from 7 to 17 mm. Spanners come with open or closed ends, the latter also known as ring or box spanners. It is best to have ones that offer both on the same tool, open at one end and closed at the other. A 150-mm (6-inch) long adjustable spanner, which has an opening capacity of 20 mm, will also be useful.

Screwdrivers

A medium Phillips cross-head (size 2) and two flat-head screwdrivers, one 3 mm and the other 6 mm.

Needle-nose Pliers

These are used for holding and pulling cables.

The MTB-3 Rescue Tool from Park Tools includes a chain tool (bottom) along with a range of screwdrivers, spanners (wrenches) and Allen keys (hex wrenches).

Cable Cutter

You can get a specialized cutting tool for bicycle cables and their housings.

Chain Tool

This is used to separate and reconnect a chain, replace broken links or shorten a new chain.

Top Tip

Have a look in your home or car toolbox, as it may already contain many of the tools that you will need to maintain your bicycle.

Lubricant

Do not use general-purpose oil. Buy a liquid bicycle lubricant suitable for the chain. This will also lubricate most other parts. Environmentally friendly lubricants and wax are available, like those produced by Green Oil.

Grease

If you are likely to be adjusting the height of the seatpost, or working on headsets, hubs or brackets, you will need bicycle grease and special grease for carbon seatposts.

Solvent

You can get environmentally friendly chain cleaners like Green Oil's Clean Chain Degreaser, which can be diluted to clean other parts of the bike, or you can use a citrus-based solvent.

Puncture-repair Kit

A repair kit with a separate adhesive is better for a strong bond than self-adhesive patches.

Ruler

A good ruler with inches marked on it is used for measuring the chain.

Tyre Levers

These are used to lever the tyre from the rim for puncture repair or replacing an inner tube.

Bicycle Pump

It is best to get two: one frame pump, hand or mini-pump for when you are out and about and a track pump with a pressure gauge for home use. The important thing is to get one with the right valve attachment. You can get an adaptor if necessary. There are two types of valve. If it is 6 mm in diameter and threaded from top to bottom, it is a Presta valve. If it is 8 mm in diameter and threaded only halfway from the top, it is a Schrader valve.

Bicycle Work Stand

Though expensive for a good one, if you do intend to maintain your bicycle properly you will find it very useful.

Extra Tools

Apart from the tools listed, you may also need a few more specialist tools if you want to go that little bit further with your maintenance and repairs. These will be mentioned when those tasks are covered.

NEW BIKE TASKS

When you get a new bicycle (brand new or used), you will want to make sure that your saddle is set at the right height and you may also want to add lights, mudguards and a rack. These are covered here before we look at cleaning, lubricating and tyre and puncture repair. See page 149 for a labelled photo showing the parts of a bike, in case you are unfamiliar with them.

Seat Height

Your seat should be set so that your knee is slightly bent when the pedal is at its lowest point. To adjust the height, loosen the securing bolt at the top of the frame tube. You can do this with a spanner or Allen key, depending on the type of nut that has been used. Once loose, you can adjust the seatpost before firmly retightening.

Lights

These are very easy to attach, usually coming with a bracket that clamps to the handlebars or frame with a screw and the light clips on to this. Dynamo-powered lights are a little trickier, but not much.

Dynamos

There are two types of dynamo: hub dynamos that are part of a wheel and bottle dynamos that attach to a frame fork and sit against a wheel.

⚙ **Hub dynamo**: As these are already built into a wheel, all you need do is replace your existing wheel with the dynamo wheel and connect it to the lights.

⚙ **Bottle dynamo**: Most probably you will need to buy a separate dynamo bracket as well as your dynamo. The bracket is first fitted to a wheel fork of your frame by clamping around it, and the bottle dynamo is then attached to the bracket. Once in place you can connect it to the lights.

Above: Attaching a dynamo light to the frame.
Below: Attaching a bottle dynamo to its bracket.

Mudguards

If your bicycle has holes in the forks where the wheel is attached, these are for attaching the metal struts of mudguards and pannier racks. If there is a hole in the centre of the frame at the crown of the forks, the top of the mudguard is screwed in here. If there are no holes, you can buy mudguards with their own mounting systems.

Pannier Racks

These attach at the base in the same place as mudguards and can share the same hole. At the top, some racks are designed to be screwed into place using two holes on each fork. If your bicycle doesn't have these holes, you will need to get a rack with its own mounting system.

Above: Attaching a mudguard at the base – the same hole can be shared by the pannier rack.

Below: Here you can see the mudguard and pannier rack top mounts.

Top Tip

If you don't want to damage the paintwork on your bicycle when attaching a metal clamp, you can cut a piece of old inner tube to the right size and place it around the frame before mounting the bracket on top.

CLEANING AND LUBRICATING

A monthly clean and lubrication will help keep your machine in prime condition. It is very important that you clean before you lubricate, especially the chain, otherwise oil will carry dirt deeper into the moving parts, doing more harm than good.

Cleaning the Frame

1. Place your bicycle on the work stand if you have one or lean it against a wall.

2. Wipe the bicycle with warm water except for the chain and the parts it contacts. If the bicycle is very dirty, or for the dirtier areas, you can use a citrus degreaser. Leave it for two minutes and rinse off. Wipe off the moisture with a clean, dry cloth.

Cleaning the frame with a proprietary cleaner.

3. Apply polish or wax to the paintwork and any chrome parts if you wish. Wax will protect the paint and prevent chrome from rusting. Avoid getting harsh cleaning products on the tyres and brake pads. Also avoid getting lubricant or wax on the rims and brake pads.

Top Tip

Rather than buy new cloths and brushes for cleaning, reuse old washing-up sponges, old clothing and old toothbrushes and nailbrushes.

The Parts of a Bicycle

Seat · Stem · Handlebar · Headset · Shifter · Seatpost · Frame (Top Tube) · Brake Lever · Seatpost Clamp · Head Tube · Seat Tube · Front Brake · Rear Brake · Down Tube · Fork · Seat Stay · Front Derailleur · Tyre · Brake Cable · Spoke · Hub · Rim · Cogset · Rear Derailleur · Crank Arm · Chain · Pedal · Chain Stay · Chainring · Valve

The Chain Drive

The key area to suffer wear is the chain and those parts it comes into contact with. Dirt is the prime culprit, so cleaning before lubricating is essential. Depending on the type of bicycle you have, there will be different parts with different names so, for the purpose of keeping this simple, I am calling the whole area the 'chain drive'. This comprises the following:

⚙ **The chain:** This connects the pedals to the rear wheel.

⚙ **The chainrings:** These are the sprockets (cogs) by the pedals.

⚙ **The cogset:** This is the set of sprockets on the rear wheel.

⚙ **Derailleurs:** These are the attachments by the chainring and cogset that push the chain from one sprocket to another.

Wiping the chain.

Cleaning between sprockets.

Applying degreaser to a derailleur.

Using a brush to help get between sprockets.

Cleaning the Chain Drive

Most of the time you can clean this area whilst the chain is on the bicycle. You can buy a special chain cleaning tool if you wish, but the steps below use brushes and cloths.

1. Place your bicycle on a work stand or upside down if you don't have one.

2. Brush some clean, warm water into the chain and everything it has contact with – the chainrings, cogsets and derailleurs. Hold a damp cloth around the chain and pedal backwards.

3. Next make a fold in the cloth and work it, back and forth, in between the sprockets. Don't expect to get all the dirt off at this stage.

4. With a clean brush, work some solvent or degreaser into all parts of the chain drive.

Top Tip

If you want to make sure your chain is thoroughly dry, you can give it a few minutes with a hairdryer.

Toothbrushes or nailbrushes are great for the chain, derailleurs and the tops of the sprockets, whilst a longer, stiff-bristled brush is ideal for getting in between the sprockets. Alternatively, use a clean cloth, folded and worked in between the sprockets.

5. Using some warm water, a clean brush and a clean cloth, remove any degreaser and dirt, making sure to get in between each chain link and the sprockets.

6. Finally, dry anywhere that has got wet, with a clean, dry cloth.

Lubricating and Greasing

Oiling the chain.

This simply involves spraying or dripping lubricant to the relevant parts and then operating them to aid penetration. After a minute wipe off the excess. GripShift gears, hubs, headsets, bottom brackets and pivot points need greasing annually, unless they incorporate sealed or cartridge bearings which require no maintenance. Some of these jobs involve a high degree of competency and more tools so, if you are unsure, have a mechanic do it. The following are easy ones.

The Chain

Apply lubricant sparingly on each link as you pedal backwards. Wipe off any excess.

Cables

The inner wires should be oiled every few months by unclipping the outer housing and dripping or spraying oil into the hole at the end, then sliding the housing up and down the inner wire a few times.

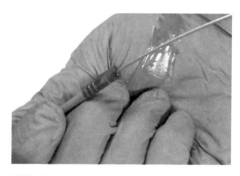

Cable lubrication.

Lubricating the rear derailleur.

Brakes

Lubricate the pivot points. Do not get oil on the brake pads or rims as this can damage the pads and lead to brake failure.

Derailleurs

Lubricate the pivot points on the derailleurs, front and back. Also, on the rear, apply a little lubricant to the centre of the derailleur pulleys.

Pedals

Clipless pedals that lock on to an attachment (cleat) on the rider's shoe should be scrubbed clean with warm soapy water and given a light spray with lubricant. For ordinary platform pedals, drip oil on to the rotating areas, spin them round and wipe off any excess. Be aware that oil on the pedals can be transferred to your shoes and from there on to carpets!

Freewheels

There are two kinds of cogset: a 'freewheel' and the newer, more common 'cassette'. If you have a freewheel this can be oiled every few months. To tell the difference look at the outer end of your cogset; a freewheel will be open and you can see inside, but a cassette will appear closed. To oil the freewheel, hold the rear end of the bicycle off the ground, tipped at an angle of about 45 degrees. Turn the pedals a few times to get the wheel spinning. Drip a little oil into the open end of the freewheel and keep turning for 10 seconds after you have stopped oiling and then wipe off any excess.

A cassette cogset.

Seatposts

To prevent this from seizing, apply a little grease twice a year. Carbon seatposts need a special lubricant. Check with your bicycle's manufacturer.

A freewheel cogset.

PUNCTURE REPAIR & MORE

In this section we focus on the tyre, as you are likely to be most keen to know how to repair a puncture. But it is also important to regularly check for loose nuts, cracks in the frame, broken or loose spokes, damaged cables, worn brake pads and wheel buckles. This is something that you should do more regularly than once a month, with some checks before every ride. Here we cover some key areas, with links to more help.

Removing Wheels

Many maintenance tasks require a wheel to be removed and to do that you will first need to unhook the brakes to make enough room.

Unhooking cantilever brakes.

Unhooking Brakes

⚙ **Cantilever brakes:** These can usually be disengaged by unhooking the straddling wire.

⚙ **V-brakes:** These can be lifted out of their cradle.

Unhooking V-brakes.

⚙ **Caliper brakes:** These sometimes have a small lever at the brake end of the cable, which will disengage the cable when lifted.

⚙ **Adjustment barrel:** If you have a problem unhooking your brakes, you may be able to use the adjustment barrel to loosen them enough to get the wheel through, especially if you

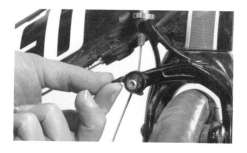
Unhooking caliper brakes.

deflate the tyre a little. The adjustment barrel is a narrow tube with a locknut at the end of the brake cable, usually by the brake lever. Loosen the locknut by hand and screw the barrel towards the locknut to loosen the brakes.

Pinch bolt: If the adjustment barrel is already fully turned or doesn't turn enough, you will need to undo the cable's pinch bolt. This is the bolt that holds the end of the cable near the brake. This is a last resort as it can be a fiddle to reattach.

Using the adjustment barrel to loosen a brake.

Undoing a brake cable's pinch bolt.

The Front Wheel

1. With the brakes disengaged, place the bicycle on the work stand or turn it upside down.

2. The wheel will be held between the forks with either nuts or a quick-release mechanism. The latter has an arm extending from it that you can pull to release the wheel. If it is held with nuts, you can loosen them with appropriate-sized spanners. If they are very tight, spray some lubricant on them. You can now remove the wheel.

3. To replace the wheel, guide the axle into the slots in the forks. These slots are called dropouts.

4. If securing the wheel with nuts, make sure the washer is on the outside of the fork. Tighten each nut a little at a time, alternating between the two. For quick-release, turn the knob clockwise with the lever in the open position, then close it. It should close firmly but not be so stiff that it is a struggle. If it is tough, release it and turn the knob slightly anticlockwise.

5. Make sure the wheel is aligned between the forks and test it is secure by hitting the side of the tyre with the palm of your hand. It should not slip to the side.

6. Reconnect the front brake and check to make sure the pads are aligned correctly. If you deflated the tyre then reinflate it.

The Rear Wheel

1. Shift your gears so that the chain is on the smallest sprockets, front and rear.

2. Release the brakes in the same way as described for the front wheel.

Using the quick-release mechanism to remove a wheel.

3. Pull back the derailleur if you have one and open the quick-release, or loosen the securing nuts, then remove the wheel.

4. To replace the wheel, guide the chain on to the smallest sprocket and the axle into the fork dropouts. Once in place tighten with the quick-release mechanism or nuts in the same way as for the front wheel, making sure it is aligned and secure.

Top Tip

After removing a wheel smear a little grease or rub some oil on the threads to make it easier to remove in future.

5. Reattach the brakes and make sure they are properly aligned. If you deflated the tyre then reinflate it.

Tyres

Make sure that tyres are inflated to the correct pressure. Examine each tyre for embedded glass, thorns or other debris and, if you find any, remove them. Also check the tyre tread and sidewalls for wear, cuts and bulges. If you have any large cuts or tears, it is best to replace the tyre.

Changing a Tyre

1. Remove the wheel as described at the beginning of this section and deflate the tyre by pressing on the inner part of the valve.

2. Ease a tyre lever between the tyre and the wheel rim, then press it down against the edge of the rim, taking care not to puncture the inner tube. This should lift the inner edge of the tyre out of the wheel well. Hook the other end of the lever around a spoke.

3. Do the same with a second tyre lever about an eighth of the way around the rim but, instead of securing it to a spoke, slide it along the rim away from the first lever. This should bring the edge of the tyre all the way off. Now you can completely remove the whole tyre from the rim.

Using a second tyre lever to fully separate the tyre from the rim – it can then be removed completely.

4. Fit one side of the new tyre into the rim and ease the inner tube into it. This is easiest if the inner tube is partially inflated. Make sure that no part of the tube is protruding under the edge.

5. Starting near the valve, work the edge of the tyre over the rim with your hands. Towards the end the tyre will become tightly stretched. At this point use your tyre levers, working from either side towards the centre, prising the last part over the rim.

6. Check both sides of the rim all the way around to make sure that no part of the inner tube is trapped, then inflate slowly to begin with, whilst checking that the inner tube is not pinched. Replace the wheel.

Replacing an Inner Tube

1. Follow the steps for changing a tyre until one edge of the tyre is off the wheel, but don't remove the whole tyre.

2. Remove the inner tube valve from the hole and remove the old inner tube from inside the tyre.

3. Insert the valve of the new inner tube and feed the rest of the tube into the tyre.

4. Continue to fit the tyre, following the instructions for changing a tyre.

Removing an inner tube.

Repairing a Puncture

Punctures are usually caused by a sharp object penetrating the tyre from the outside, although sometimes they can be caused by a spoke pushing through from inside the wheel rim, or by brakes dragging on the side of the tyre.

1. Remove the wheel as described at the start of this section and examine the tyre to see what might have caused the damage. If you do find something, remove it and mark the tyre with the small crayon or chalk that comes with your repair kit. If you don't find any obvious cause for the puncture, just continue with the steps.

Marking the damage.

2. Remove one edge of the tyre as described earlier.

3. Remove the inner tube from inside the tyre, but leave the valve in the wheel. If you found a potential cause for the puncture and marked the location with a crayon, you will now be able to check the inside of the tyre for anything sticking through and look at the inner tube to see if there is a puncture at that point.

Sanding the puncture.

Gluing the area to be covered.

Sticking on the patch.

Top Tip

At night, in heavy rain or both together it can be easier to replace an inner tube than fix a puncture. Carry a spare inner tube with you and repair the puncture back at home.

4. Whether you found a hole or not, partially inflate the tube, hold it close to your ear and slide it through your hands, listening for a hiss. If you hear something but can't identify the exact spot when you move it away from your ear, dab some water or spit on the tube in the approximate area and watch for bubbles. Alternatively, feed the tube under water in a bucket. When you have located the puncture, mark the spot with your crayon.

5. Dry the inner tube and roughen the area around the hole with sandpaper, then spread glue around the puncture covering an area a little larger than the size of the patch you are going to use. Leave the glue a few moments to become tacky.

6. Place the patch over the puncture, pressing it down firmly, before peeling off the plastic cover. Dust the area with grated chalk and wait five minutes to make sure the glue is properly dry, then replace the inner tube and tyre as described earlier.

Wheels

These should be properly secured and aligned centrally between the forks with no lean to either side. Broken spokes should be replaced. Check for kinks and warps in the rim by spinning the wheel and watching the rim as it passes the brake pads. If you notice any wobbles, it is best to have an expert carry out the repairs. Visit www.flametree publishing.com/extras for how to check and tighten loose hubs.

Tightening the hub locknut.

The Chain

Chains will wear and 'stretch' over time, especially if not lubricated regularly. This can wear down the chainrings and cogsets leading to chain slippage, poor performance and possible accidents.

Checking the Chain for Wear

Wear on the chain is caused by dirt getting into its joints, combined with the constant friction of contact with the sprockets. A chain-wear indicator tool can be bought cheaply, but you can simply use a ruler instead. Each chain link is made exactly half an inch long, so 12 inches from

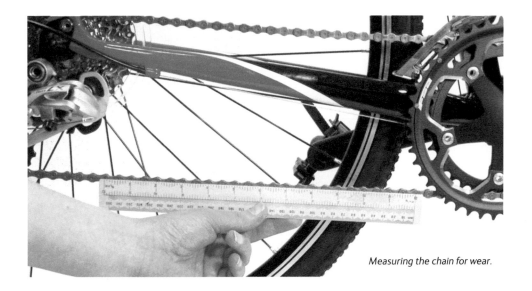

Measuring the chain for wear.

the centre of a link pin should be the centre of the 24th pin along. If the chain is longer by more than 1/16 inch, then it is time to replace it. Visit www.flametreepublishing.com/extras for how to replace a worn chain.

Sprockets

A worn chain will compound wear on the sprockets. As sprockets wear, the teeth become more pointed with wider gaps between them, giving a wave-like appearance. Check the chainrings and cogsets for worn, bent, chipped or missing teeth. If this is the case with any of your sprockets, it is best to change the whole set.

Top Tip

Keep a note of the distance you have covered with a new chain. It should be good for at least 800 km (500 miles). After that, check it regularly for chain stretch.

Pedals

Make sure the pedals are securely attached to the crank arms. Try to move a pedal from side to side whilst firmly holding the crank arm. If there is movement, there may be a problem with the bearings inside the pedal. Hold a pedal so that it remains level whilst you rotate the crank arm one full circle. Any stickiness or roughness indicates a bearing problem. Have it checked by a mechanic.

Cranks

These join the crank arms inside the bicycle frame. There are three kinds: one piece, cottered and cotterless. The first does not need checking but the other two do. Wiggle the crank arms from side to side. There should be no movement. You can also use your hands to press down hard on to the pedals, then rotate them 180 degrees and press again. If you hear a click, one of the cranks may be loose. Visit www.flametreepublishing.com/extras for how to tighten cranks.

Using an Allen key to tighten the crank.

Brakes

There are many types of braking system for bicycles. The most common are rim brakes. Of these there are three main types: caliper, cantilever and V-brakes. They are all essentially operated by levers on the handlebars that pull arms on either side of each wheel via a cable. On the ends of the arms are pads that close on the wheel rim to cause braking by friction. Visit www.flametreepublishing.com/extras for how to properly check your brakes and replace brake pads, adjust and tighten brakes and more brake maintenance.

Loosening the lever-arm nut in order to adjust a break pad.

Gears

Your gears should change smoothly and easily without the chain jumping off. If they don't, the chain may have some stiff links. Check them by moving each link by hand. If any are stiff, clean

Loosening the front derailleur clamp in order to adjust the gears.

the chain and lubricate, working the stiff links by hand until they are flexible. If the chain is fine and the gear changes are poor, it can be caused by damaged sprocket teeth so check these too. If all is well with the chain and sprockets, and your gears still skip, then you will need to adjust them. Visit www.flametreepublishing.com/extras for how to adjust the gears.

Loosening the headset locknut.

Handlebars and Headset

Check that the handlebars are not bent or cracked. If they are, you will need to replace them. Also check that they are secure by holding the wheel firmly and trying to move the handlebars from side to side, forwards and backwards. If there is any movement, tighten the bolts that secure them.

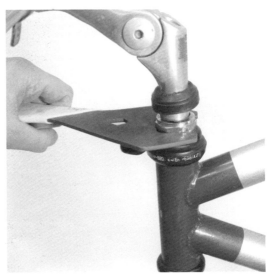

The headset is the part of the bicycle that connects the front fork to the frame and allows the forks to be turned by the handlebars. The handlebar and front wheel should roll easily to one side when the front of the bike is lifted. If not, the headset will need loosening. And if it makes a clicking sound when the bike is braked and rocked back and forth it is too loose. Visit www.flametreepublishing.com/extras for how to adjust headsets.

Saddle and Seatpost

The saddle should be horizontal, although some have a slight incline for reasons of comfort. You can make adjustments to the angle by loosening the nuts beneath the saddle and tilting it accordingly.

The seatpost needs to be greased every six months to a year. Loosen the bolt at the top of the frame tube with either a spanner or Allen key, slide the seatpost out and wipe some grease on the post before reinserting it to the correct height, then tightening the securing bolt.

CHECKLIST

⚙ **Tools:** Make sure you have the basic tools and items necessary for cleaning and maintaining your bicycle – basic adjustments are easier than you might think, especially with the appropriate tools!

⚙ **New bike tasks:** Make sure your saddle is set at the right height and that you have added any necessary or useful items such as lights, mudguards and a rack.

⚙ **Clean then lubricate:** Clean your bicycle, including degreasing the chain drive and rinsing, before lubricating. Wipe off excess oil especially from the chain and surrounding area.

⚙ **Removing wheels:** Learn how to unhook brakes and remove the front and rear wheels – you'll need to be able to do this before making any repairs to the tyres or inner tubes.

⚙ **Replacing tyres and inner tubes:** Using a tyre lever to remove a tyre makes it much simpler. You will also then be able to replace the inner tube if necessary.

⚙ **Punctures:** Remove the inner tube as described and easily patch up any pesky punctures.

⚙ **Test:** After making any adjustments, test your bicycle somewhere safe before going on the road.

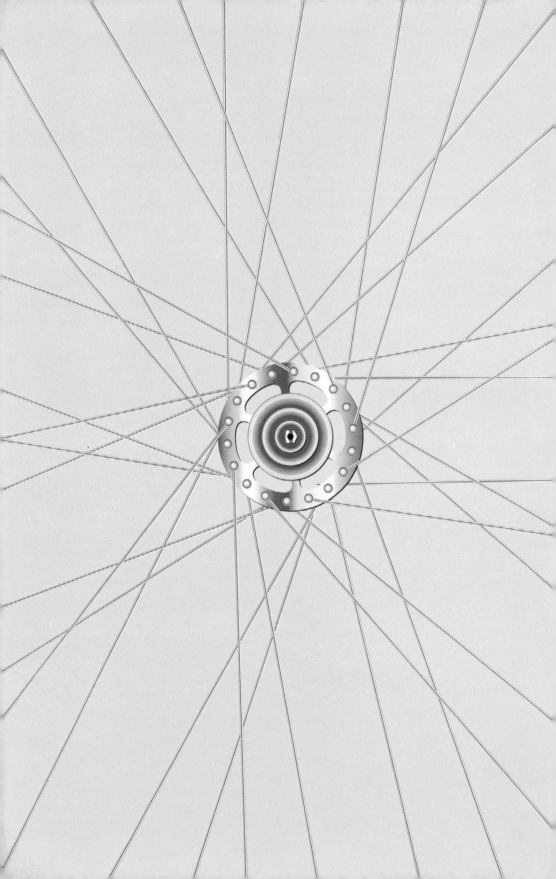

TROUBLESHOOTING

YOUR BODY

Once you have adjusted to the routine of cycling, you should be able to ride comfortably without suffering any aches or pains. If you do experience any discomfort, use this troubleshooting guide to find the solution.

Ankles and Feet

Pain in the tendons at the back of your ankles is usually caused by the position of your foot on the pedal. Either your seat is a little too high or, if you are using clipless pedals (see page 152), they may be set too far forward. It is also possible that you may have a damaged pedal or crank. Soreness in the balls of the feet is due to the pressure exerted whilst pedalling.

Solution

- **Bike adjustment:** Check the pedals and cranks to make sure they are undamaged and properly secured. Make adjustments to your seat height or pedals, and tighten loose shoe cleats as these can also cause ankle problems over time.

- **Shoes:** Use thicker-soled shoes to prevent soreness of the balls of the feet.

Back

The most common cause of back pain whilst cycling is due to poor posture compounded by jolts, particularly on rough roads or tracks.

Solution

- **Posture:** Your back should be arched out from the hips to the shoulders, and your shoulders rounded. In this way jolts will be dissipated across your back, but if your back is curved in, the energy of the shocks will be more focused into the small of your back.

⚙ **Suspension:** For those using bicycles with a more upright riding position, or are riding off-road without suspension, the solution is to get a sprung leather saddle. You can also stand on the pedals for particularly bumpy surfaces. All cyclists, road or off-road, should make sure that tyres are inflated to the correct pressure.

Fingers, Hands and Wrists

Numbness in the fingers that is not related to the cold is likely to be caused by pressure on the dip between the pads at the base of the palm, caused by too much padding or holding the handlebars incorrectly. Soreness of the palm is due to too little padding and wrist pain is due to posture.

Solution

⚙ **Padding:** If you are wearing gloves with a lot of padding, especially at the base of the palm, change them. If your handlebar grips are padded in such a way that pressure on them can cause the padding to mould to your hand, replace them with firmer ones.

⚙ **Hand position:** Make sure that you are not putting too much weight on to the base of the palm. Adjust your hand position to spread the weight and make sure your wrist is not dipped or raised but is aligned to your forearm. Check your handlebar height. It should not be more than an inch lower than the saddle, ideally at the same height.

Knees

Knee pain and injury can occur for various reasons, all of which relate to your posture or pedalling technique. A saddle that is too low or too high will cause strain on your knees, as will pedalling with undue force.

⚙ **Posture:** Make sure that your saddle is at the right height so that when you pedal your knee is slightly bent when the pedal is at its lowest point. Your hips should not move from side to side. If they do, you have probably set the saddle too high.

⚙ **Technique:** Pressure can be placed on the knee if you pedal in too high a gear. You should not feel that you have to force the pedal. Also, check that your knees do not move to the sides when you pedal.

Neck and Shoulders

Neck problems are usually due to the head being tilted back too far and are most likely to affect riders with a forward-leaning posture. Shoulder pain is caused by poor posture and may well be due to a saddle being tilted too far forward.

Solution

Make sure your handlebars are not set too low and make adjustments to their angle if necessary. If your back is not arched and your shoulders are not rounded, this will also cause the neck to dip and compress the vertebrae. Correcting your posture will also alleviate shoulder pain. Make sure that you ride with a slight bend in your elbows and that your shoulders and back are rounded. Raise the saddle slightly if it is tilted down at the front.

Thighs and Buttocks

If you experience muscle aches after short rides, you are probably pedalling in too high a gear. Soreness of the buttocks or base of the spine will be due to poor posture, a poor saddle or both. Chafing will be due to your clothing or rolling your hips from side to side as you pedal.

Solution

- **Saddle and padding**: Traditional leather saddles are best for preventing chafing and sprung saddles will provide suspension. Saddles come in different shapes and sizes and are typically divided according to gender. Make sure you are using the right type of saddle for you. Cycling shorts, trousers and underwear will not have seams in places that are likely to rub and they may also include some padding.

- **Posture and technique:** Make sure you are sitting properly and that you do not slide from side to side on the saddle as you pedal.

YOUR BICYCLE

This section looks at the most common mechanical problems that can arise whilst you are cycling, the symptoms of which are usually a noise if the problem is chronic, or a sudden failure, like your chain coming off.

Wheel Noise

⚙ **Constant sound:** This will be a misaligned brake pad, a wheel that is not centred properly, a tyre that is not fitted correctly, a mudguard that is misaligned or some trapped debris like a leaf. Check these and adjust as necessary.

⚙ **Once per revolution:** A sound that occurs once every time the wheel goes round is most likely to be an irregularity on the rim brushing against the brake pad. You will need to have the wheel trued (aligned correctly).

Creaking and clicking: Check for loose or broken spokes. Squeeze the spokes in pairs to see if you can duplicate the noise. It they make the noise but are not loose or broken, lubricate. If any are loose or broken, they will need tightening or replacing.

The hub: If none of the above is the cause of the noise, the problem will most likely be the wheel hub. Tighten the hub and if it still makes a noise, the bearings may need a service.

Rear wheel only: If the noise comes from the rear wheel only, and only in certain gears, check the sprockets for wear or damage. Replace as necessary.

Pedal Noise

Once per revolution: This is most likely to be caused by a loose crank. Modern cotterless cranks can be tightened quite easily. Visit www.flametreepublishing.com/extras. If the crank frequently comes loose, it will need to be replaced.

Creaking: This is most likely to be a loose crank.

Screeching: This will be due to bearings that are dry or damaged.

Pedals: If the actual pedals are making a noise, check they are attached properly and lubricate them. If the noise persists, have a mechanic look at them.

Chainrings: The bolts on these might be loose or the noise might only occur as you change gear. Check the chainring for wear or damage to the teeth, and make sure they are securely fitted to each other and the bottom bracket.

Chain Noise

Once per revolution: This will be caused by a damaged or stiff chain. Lubrication and some flexing of the chain should free stiff links. If links are damaged, then they, or the chain, will need to be replaced.

Chain slap: This is where the chain slaps against the frame. If you have a freewheel, it may need adjusting. Some chain slap is normal, but if you find it excessive and the freewheel is not the cause, the rear derailleur will need adjusting.

Other Noises

Rattling: This is generally due to something being loose. Check that all nuts and bolts are tight. Check any attachments and accessories like lights, the bell, racks and mudguards.

Creaking: This is usually due to lack of lubrication. If the handlebars creak, you need to make sure the clamp bolt is lubricated and tight. If creaking of the handlebars persists, have your bicycle checked by a mechanic before riding it as it might lead to a steering failure.

Screeching: If this occurs when you apply the brakes you will need to toe them in. Visit www.flametreepublishing.com/extras.

Mechanical Failure

Most mechanical failure is obvious, as is the solution, but there are a few problems for which the solutions are not apparent. The following are the main ones that could be hazardous.

Chain Suck

This is where your chain does not shift properly and gets trapped between two chainrings. This is caused by wear and damage to the chainring teeth or the chain. Worn or damaged chainrings need to be replaced. Damaged chain links need to be replaced. Make sure the chain has not stretched and regularly clean and lubricate it, as well as the chainrings, cogset and derailleurs if you have them. See pages 150–52 and visit www.flametreepublishing.com/extras.

Chain Slip

If your chain ever slips off the chainrings, you can feed it back on by hand, under and over. If your chain repeatedly comes off (and it is clean and lubricated), it is either too loose, probably due to being stretched, so will need replacing, or the derailleurs are not properly adjusted. Which sprockets the chain comes off will determine which derailleurs need adjustment, front or rear. See page 150–52 and visit www.flametreepublishing.com/extras.

Brake Failure (Rim Brakes)

- **Levers:** If the brake lever depresses further than it should, you will need to inspect the brake cable. It might have come loose, most likely at the brake end, snapped or, if the problem is chronic, then the cable has probably stretched. Adjust or replace as necessary.

- **Slow stopping:** If the cables are taut and the levers are working, the brake arm mechanisms may be sticking. Test by looking at them when you depress the brake. They should hinge freely. If they don't, they will need cleaning and lubricating. If they close properly, your brake pads may be worn or misaligned. If the pads are not worn, and are meeting the rim as they should, there is probably oil on the pads and/or rims. Degrease the rims with a citrus-based solvent or alcohol and replace both pads.

CHECKLIST

Posture: Develop a good cycling posture, with a rounded back and arms slightly bent at the elbows to help prevent pain or injury from the jolts of riding.

Sit up: Make sure that you have your saddle at the right height for you. It will aid your posture, improve your efficiency and keep your knees and back from suffering pain and injury.

Reach: Have your handlebars at a similar height to your saddle and angle your brake levers so that your fingers extend to them in line with the slope of your arms.

Low gear: Pedalling quickly in a lower gear will take the strain off your knees and thigh muscles.

Service: Giving your bicycle a regular check over will help to prevent many potential mechanical problems from ever arising.

Clean and lubricate: Regularly clean and lubricate your bicycle's moving parts to keep them moving freely.

Get help: If in doubt about any problem, whether it's an ache in your back or a clunk in your bicycle, then ask an expert for help. That's what they're for.

FURTHER READING & WEBSITES

British Medical Association, *Cycling: Towards Health and Safety*, Wiley-Blackwell, 1992

Franklin, J., *Cyclecraft: The Complete Guide to Safe and Enjoyable Cycling for Adults and Children*, Stationery Office, 2008

Friel, J., *Cycling Past 50*, Human Kinetics, 2002

Friel, J., *The Cyclist's Training Bible*, Velo Press, 2009

Furia, E., *The Big Book of Bicycling*, Rodale Press, 2010

McMullen, R., *Cycling to Work: A Beginner's Guide*, Green Books, 2007

Park Tools., *Big Blue Book of Bicycle Repair*, Park Tools, 2009

Peveler, W., *The Complete Book of Road Cycling & Racing: A Manual for the Dedicated Rider*, Ragged Mountain Press, 2008

Pruitt, A., *Complete Medical Guide for Cyclists*, Velo Press, 2006

Root, J., *The World of BMX*, Motorbooks International, 2003

Salter, P., *Bike Britain: Cycling from Land's End to John O' Groats*, Vine House, 2003

Sidwells, C., *Complete Bike Book*, Dorling Kindersley, 2003

Smith, D., *Cycling for Fitness*, A & C Black, 2001

Vance, P., *Bicycle Touring: The Complete Book on Touring by Bike*, Van der Plas Publications, 2006

Van der Plas, Rob, *Simple Bicycle Repair. Fixing Your Bike Made Easy*, Van der Plas Publications, 2006

Worland, S., *The Mountain Bike Book*, J.H. Haynes & Co Ltd, 2003

www.bikeradar.com
A very informative site on all things cycling, including a public forum.

www.bikeregister.com
An online registration initiative aiming to reduce bicycle theft and assist owner recovery.
www.nationalbikeregistry.com in the USA

www.bikewebsite.com/bikeopedia.htm
A very useful glossary of bicycle terms and jargon. The rest of the website also provides information on bicycle maintenance.

www.britishcycling.org.uk
The national governing body for cycling in the UK promoting cycling as a sport, recreation and sustainable transport.

www.cptips.com
Lots of tips for improving your cycling performance including training, nutrition and equipment.

www.ctc.org.uk
This is the website for the UK's national cyclists' organization, CTC, who have been protecting and promoting the rights of cyclists since 1878. They have an excellent members' forum.

www.cyclechat.net
An online forum with topics on sports, commuting and choosing a bicycle.

www.parktool.com/blog/repair-help
A very well organized and accessible site for maintenance advice and tips.

www.sheldonbrown.com
The Sheldon Brown website is a goldmine of maintenance and technical knowledge, beautifully explained and very comprehensive.

www.usacycling.org
USA Cycling is a family of organizations that promotes and governs different disciplines of cycling sports.

www.whycycle.co.uk
A very practical and easy-to-read site covering all aspects of cycling, including cycling with children, cycling with disability and safety.

INDEX